Manifesta Coffee Break

1943

We Refugees

By Hannah Arendt

IN the first place, we don't like to be called "refugees." We ourselves call each other "newcomers" or "immigrants." Our newspapers are papers for "Americans of German language"; and, as far as I know, there is not and never was any club founded by Hitler-persecuted people whose name indicated that its members were refugees.

A refugee used to be a person driven to seek refuge because of some act committed or some political opinion held. Well, it is true we have had to seek refuge; but we committed no acts and most of us never dreamt of having any radical political opinion. With us the meaning of the term "refugee" has changed. Now "refugees" are those of us who have been so unfortunate as to arrive in a new country without means and have to be helped by Refugee Committees.

Before this war broke out we were even more sensitive about being called refugees. We did our best to prove to other people that we were just ordinary immigrants. We declared that we had departed of our own free will to countries of our choice, and we denied that our situation had anything to do with "so-called Jewish problems." Yes, we were "immigrants" or "newcomers" who had left our country because, one fine day, it no longer suited us to stay, or for purely economic reasons. We wanted to rebuild our lives, that was all. In order to rebuild one's life one has to be strong and an optimist. So we are very optimistic.

Our optimism, indeed, is admirable, even if we say so ourselves. The story of our struggle has finally become known. We lost our home, which means the familiarity of daily life. We lost our occupation, which means the confidence that we are of some use in this world. We lost our language, which means the naturalness of reactions, the simplicity of gestures, the unaffected expression of feelings. We left our relatives in the Polish ghettos and our best friends have been killed in concentration camps, and that means the rupture of our private lives.

Nevertheless, as soon as we were saved—and most of us had to be saved several times—we started our new lives and tried to follow as closely as possible all the good advice our saviors passed on to us. We were told to forget; and we forgot quicker than anybody ever could imagine.

In a friendly way we were reminded that the new country would become a new home; and after four weeks in France or six weeks in America, we pretended to be Frenchmen or Americans. The more optimistic among us would even add that their whole former life had been passed in a kind of unconscious exile and only their new country now taught them what a home really looks like. It is true we sometimes raise objections when we are told to forget about our former work; and our former ideals are usually hard to throw over if our social standard is at stake. With the language, however, we find no difficulties: after a single year optimists are convinced they speak English as well as their mother tongue; and after two years they swear solemnly that they speak English better than any other language—their German is a language they hardly remember.

In order to forget more efficiently we rather avoid any allusion to concentration or internment camps we experienced in nearly all European countries—it might be interpreted as pessimism or lack of confidence in the new homeland. Besides, how often have we been told that nobody likes to listen to all that; hell is no longer a religious belief or a fantasy, but something as real as houses and stones and trees. Apparently nobody wants to know that contemporary history has created a new kind of human beings—the kind that are put in concentration camps by their foes and in internment camps by their friends.

Even among ourselves we don't speak about this past. Instead, we have found our own way of mastering an uncertain future. Since everybody plans and wishes and hopes, so do we. Apart from these general human attitudes, however, we try to clear up the future more scientifically. After so much bad luck we want a course as sure as a gun. Therefore, we leave the earth with all its uncertainties behind and we cast our eyes up to the sky. The stars tell us— rather than the newspapers—when Hitler will be defeated and when we shall become American citizens. We think the stars more reliable advisers than all our friends; we learn from the stars when we should have lunch with our benefactors and on what day we have the best chances of filling out one of these countless questionnaires which accompany our present lives. Sometimes we don't rely even on the stars but rather on the lines of our hand or the signs of our handwriting. Thus we learn less about political events but more about our own dear selves, even though somehow psychoanalysis has gone out of fashion. Those happier times are past when bored ladies and gentlemen of high society conversed about the genial misdemeanors of their early childhood. They don't want ghost-stories any more; it is real experiences that make their flesh creep. There is no longer any need of bewitching the past; it is spellbound enough in reality. Thus, in spite of our outspoken optimism, we use all sorts of magical tricks to conjure up the spirits of the future.

I don't know which memories and which thoughts nightly dwell in our dreams. I dare not ask for information, since I, too, had rather be an optimist. But sometimes I imagine that at least nightly we think of our dead or we remember the poems we once loved. I could even understand how our friends of the West coast, during the curfew, should have had such curious notions as to believe that we are not only "prospective citizens" but present "enemy aliens." In daylight, of course, we become only "technically" enemy aliens—all refugees know this. But when technical reasons prevented you from leaving your home during the dark hours, it certainly was not easy to avoid some dark speculations about the relation between technicality and reality.

No, there is something wrong with our optimism. There are those odd optimists among us who, having made a lot of optimistic speeches, go home and turn on the gas or make use of a skyscraper in quite an unexpected way. They seem to prove that our proclaimed cheerfulness is based on a dangerous readiness for death. Brought up in the conviction that life is the highest good and death the greatest dismay, we became witnesses and victims of worse terrors than death—without having been able to discover a higher ideal than life. Thus, although death lost its horror for us, we became neither willing nor capable to risk our lives for a cause. Instead of fighting—or thinking about how to become able to fight back—refugees have got used to wishing death to friends or relatives; if somebody dies, we cheerfully imagine all the trouble he has been saved. Finally many of us end by wishing that we, too, could be saved some trouble, and act accordingly.

Since 1938—since Hitler's invasion of Austria—we have seen how quickly eloquent optimism could change to speechless pessimism. As time went on, we got worse—even more optimistic and even more inclined to suicide. Austrian Jews under Schuschnigg were such a cheerful people—all impartial observers admired them. It was quite wonderful how deeply convinced they were that nothing could happen to them. But when German troops invaded the country and Gentile neighbors started riots at Jewish homes, Austrian Jews began to commit suicide.

Unlike other suicides, our friends leave no explanation of their deed, no indictment, no charge against a world that had forced a desperate man to talk and to behave cheerfully to his very last day. Letters left by them are conventional, meaningless documents. Thus, funeral orations we make at their open graves are brief, embarrassed and very hopeful. Nobody cares about motives, they seem to be clear to all of us.

I speak of unpopular facts; and it makes things worse that in order to prove my point I do not even dispose of the sole arguments which impress modern people—figures. Even those Jews who furiously deny the existence of the Jewish people give us a fair chance of survival as far as figures are concerned—how else could they prove that only a few Jews are criminals and that many Jews are being killed as good patriots in wartime? Through their effort to save the statistical life of the Jewish people we know that Jews had the lowest suicide rate among all civilized nations. I am quite sure those figures are no longer correct, but I cannot prove it with new figures, though I can certainly with new experiences. This might be sufficient for those skeptical souls who never were quite convinced that the measure of one's skull gives the exact idea of its content, or that statistics of crime show the exact level of national ethics. Anyhow, wherever European Jews are living today, they no longer behave according to statistical laws. Suicides occur not only among the panic-stricken people in Berlin and Vienna, in Bucharest or Paris, but in New York and Los Angeles, in Buenos Aires and Montevideo.

On the other hand, there has been little reported about suicides in the ghettoes and concentration camps themselves. True, we had very few reports at all from Poland, but we have been fairly well informed about German and French concentration camps.

At the camp of Gurs, for instance, where I had the opportunity of spending some time, I heard only once about suicide, and that was the suggestion of a collective action, apparently a kind of protest in order to vex the French. When some of us remarked that we had been shipped there *"pour crever"* in any case, the general mood turned suddenly into a violent courage of life. The general opinion held that one had to be abnormally asocial and unconcerned about general events if one was still able to interpret the whole accident as personal and individual bad luck and, accordingly, ended one's life personally and individually. But the same people, as soon as they returned to their own individual lives, being faced with

seemingly individual problems, changed once more to this insane optimism which is next door to despair.

We are the first non-religious Jews persecuted—and we are the first ones who, not only *in extremis*, answer with suicide. Perhaps the philosophers are right who teach that suicide is the last and supreme guarantee of human freedom: not being free to create our lives or the world in which we live, we nevertheless are free to throw life away and to leave the world. Pious Jews, certainly, cannot realize this negative liberty; they perceive murder in suicide, that is, destruction of what man never is able to make, interference with the rights of the Creator. *Adonai nathan veadonai lakach* ("The Lord hath given and the Lord hath taken away"); and they would add: *baruch shem adonai* ("blessed be the name of the Lord"). For them suicide, like murder, means a blasphemous attack on creation as a whole. The man who kills himself asserts that life is not worth living and the world not worth sheltering him.

Yet our suicides are no mad rebels who hurl defiance at life and the world, who try to kill in themselves the whole universe. Theirs is a quiet and modest way of vanishing; they seem to apologize for the violent solution they have found for their personal problems. In their opinion, generally, political events had nothing to do with their individual fate; in good or bad times they would believe solely in their personality. Now they find some mysterious shortcomings in themselves which prevent them from getting along. Having felt entitled from their earliest childhood to a certain social standard, they are failures in their own eyes if this standard cannot be kept any longer. Their optimism is the vain attempt to keep head above water. Behind this front of cheerfulness, they constantly struggle with despair of themselves. Finally, they die of a kind of selfishness.

If we are saved we feel humiliated, and if we are helped we feel degraded. We fight like madmen for private existences with individual destinies, since we are afraid of becoming part of that miserable lot of *schnorrers* whom we, many of us former philanthropists, remember only too well. Just as once we failed to understand that the so-called *schnorrer* was a symbol of Jewish destiny and not a *shlemihl*, so today we don't feel entitled to Jewish solidarity; we cannot realize that we by ourselves are not so much concerned as the whole Jewish people. Sometimes this lack of comprehension has been strongly supported by our protectors. Thus, I remember a director of a great charity concern in Paris who, whenever he received the card of a German-Jewish intellectual with the inevitable "Dr." on it, used to exclaim at the top of his voice, "Herr Doktor, Herr Doktor, Herr Schnorrer, Herr Schnorrer!"

The conclusion we drew from such unpleasant experiences was simple enough. To be a doctor of philosophy no longer satisfied us; and we learnt that in order to build a new life, one has first to improve on the old one. A nice little fairy-tale has been invented to describe our behavior; a forlorn émigré dachshund, in his grief, begins to speak: "Once, when I was a St. Bernard . . ."

Our new friends, rather overwhelmed by so many stars and famous men, hardly understand that at the basis of all our descriptions of past splendors lies one human truth: once we were somebodies about whom people cared, we were loved by friends, and even known by landlords as paying our rent regularly. Once we could buy our food and ride in the subway without being told we were undesirable. We have become a little hysterical since newspapermen started detecting us and telling us publicly to stop being disagreeable when shopping for milk and bread. We wonder how it can be done; we already are so damnably careful in every moment of our daily lives to avoid anybody guessing who we are, what kind of passport we have, where our birth certificates were filled out—and that Hitler didn't like us. We try the best we can to fit into a world where you have to be sort of politically minded when you buy your food.

Under such circumstances, St. Bernard grows bigger and bigger. I never can forget that young man who, when expected to accept a certain kind of work, sighed out, "You don't know to whom you speak; I was Section-manager in Karstadt's [a great department store in Berlin]." But there is also the deep despair of that middle-aged man who, going through countless shifts of different committees in order to be saved, finally exclaimed, "And nobody here knows who I am!" Since nobody would treat him as a dignified human being, he began sending cables to great personalities and his big relations. He learnt quickly that in this mad world it is much easier to be accepted as a "great man" than as a human being.

The less we are free to decide who we are or to live as we like, the more we try to put up a front, to hide the facts, and to play roles. We were expelled from Germany because we were Jews. But having hardly crossed the French borderline, we were changed into "boches." We were even told that we had to accept this designation if we really were against Hitler's racial theories. During seven years we played the ridiculous role of trying to be Frenchmen—at least, prospective citizens; but at the beginning of the war we were interned as "boches" all the same. In the meantime, however, most of us had indeed become such loyal Frenchmen that we could not even criticize a French governmental order; thus we declared it was all right to be interned. We were the first "*prisonniers volontaires*" history has ever seen. After the Germans invaded the country, the French Government had only to change the name of the firm; having been jailed because we were Germans, we were not freed because we were Jews.

It is the same story all over the world, repeated again and again. In Europe the nazis confiscated our property; but in Brazil we have to pay 30% of our wealth, like the most loyal member of the *Bund der Auslandsdeutschen*. In Paris we could not leave our homes after eight o'clock because we were Jews; but in Los Angeles we are restricted because we are "enemy aliens." Our identity is changed so frequently that nobody can find out who we actually are.

Unfortunately, things don't look any better when we meet with Jews. French Jewry was absolutely convinced that all Jews coming from beyond the Rhine were what they called *Polaks*—what German Jewry called *Ostjuden*. But those Jews who really came from eastern Europe could not agree with their French brethren and called us *Jaeckes*. The sons of these *Jaecke*-haters—the second generation born in France and already duly assimilated—shared the opinion of the French Jewish upper classes. Thus, in the very same family, you could be called a *Jaecke* by the father and a *Polak* by the son.

Since the outbreak of the war and the catastrophe that has befallen European Jewry, the mere fact of being a refugee has prevented our mingling with native Jewish society, some exceptions only proving the rule. These unwritten social laws, though never publicly admitted, have the great force of public opinion. And such a silent opinion and practice is more important for our daily lives than all official proclamations of hospitality and good will.

Man is a social animal and life is not easy for him when social ties are cut off. Moral standards are much easier kept in the texture of a society. Very few individuals have the strength to conserve their own integrity if their social, political and legal status is completely confused. Lacking the courage to fight for a change of our social and legal status, we have decided instead, so many of us, to try a change of identity. And this curious behavior makes matters much worse. The confusion in which we live is partly our own work.

Some day somebody will write the true story of this Jewish emigration from Germany; and he will have to start with a description of that Mr. Cohn from Berlin who had always been a 150% German, a German super-patriot. In 1933 that Mr. Cohn found refuge in Prague and very quickly became a convinced Czech patriot—as true and as loyal a Czech patriot as he had been a German one. Time went on and about 1937 the Czech Government, already under some nazi pressure, began to expel its Jewish refugees, disregarding the fact that they felt so strongly as prospective Czech citizens. Our Mr. Cohn then went to Vienna; to adjust oneself there a definite Austrian patriotism was required. The German invasion forced Mr. Cohn out of that country. He arrived in Paris at a bad moment and he never did receive a regular residence-permit. Having already acquired a great skill in wishful thinking, he refused to take mere administrative measures seriously, convinced that he would spend his future life in France. Therefore, he prepared his adjustment to the French nation by identifying himself with "our" ancestor Vercingetorix. I think I had better not dilate on the further adventures of Mr. Cohn. As long as Mr. Cohn can't make up his mind to be what he actually is, a Jew, nobody can foretell all the mad changes he will still have to go through.

A man who wants to lose his self discovers, indeed, the possibilities of human existence, which are infinite, as infinite as is creation. But the re-covering of a new personality is as difficult—and as hopeless—as a new creation of the world. Whatever we do, whatever we pretend to be, we reveal nothing but our insane desire to be changed, not to be Jews. All our activities are directed to attain this aim: we don't want to be refugees, since we don't want to be Jews; we pretend to be English-speaking people, since German-speaking immigrants of recent years are marked as Jews; we don't call ourselves stateless, since the majority of stateless people in the world are Jews; we are willing to become loyal Hottentots, only to hide the fact that we are Jews. We don't succeed and we can't succeed; under the cover of our "optimism" you can easily detect the hopeless sadness of assimilationists.

With us from Germany the word assimilation received a "deep" philosophical meaning. You can hardly realize how serious we were about it. Assimilation did not mean the necessary adjustment to the country where we happened to be born and to the people whose language we happened to speak. We adjust in principle to everything and everybody. This attitude became quite clear to me once by the words of one of my compatriots who, apparently, knew how to express his feelings. Having just arrived in France, he founded one of these societies of adjustment in which German Jews asserted to each other that they were already Frenchmen. In his first speech he said: "We have been good Germans in Germany and therefore we shall be good Frenchmen in France." The public applauded enthusiastically and nobody laughed; we were happy to have learnt how to prove our loyalty.

If patriotism were a matter of routine or practice, we should be the most patriotic people in the world. Let us go back to our Mr. Cohn; he certainly has beaten all records. He is that ideal immigrant who always, and in every country into which a terrible fate has driven him, promptly sees and loves the native mountains. But since patriotism is not yet believed to be a matter of practice, it is hard to convince people of the sincerity of our repeated transformations. This struggle makes our own society so intolerant; we demand full affirmation within our own group because we are not in the position to obtain it from the natives. The natives, confronted with such strange beings as we are, become suspicious; from their point of view, as a rule, only a loyalty to our old countries is understandable. That makes life very bitter for us. We might overcome this suspicion if we would explain that, being Jews, our patriotism in our original countries had rather a peculiar aspect. Though it was indeed sincere and deep-rooted. We wrote big volumes to prove it; paid an entire bureaucracy to explore its antiquity and to explain it statistically. We had scholars write philosophical dissertations on the predestined harmony between Jews and Frenchmen, Jews and Germans, Jews and Hungarians, Jews and . . . Our so frequently suspected loyalty of today has a long history. It is the history of a hundred and fifty years of assimilated Jewry who performed an unprecedented feat: though proving all the time their non-Jewishness, they succeeded in remaining Jews all the same.

The desperate confusion of these Ulysses-wanderers who, unlike their great prototype, don't know who they are is easily explained by their perfect mania for refusing to keep their identity. This mania is much older than the last ten years which revealed the profound absurdity of our existence. We are like people with a fixed idea who can't help trying continually to disguise an imaginary stigma. Thus we are enthusiastically fond of every new possibility which, being new, seems able to work miracles. We are fascinated by every new nationality in the same way as a woman of tidy size is delighted with every new dress which promises to give her the desired waistline. But she likes the new dress only as long as she believes in its miraculous qualities, and she will throw it away as soon as she discovers that it does not change her stature—or, for that matter, her status.

One may be surprised that the apparent uselessness of all our odd disguises has not yet been able to discourage us. If it is true that men seldom learn from history, it is also true that they may learn from personal experiences which, as in our case, are repeated time and again. But before you cast the first stone at us, remember that being a Jew does not give any legal status in this world. If we should start telling the truth that we are nothing but Jews, it would mean that we expose ourselves to the fate of human beings who, unprotected by any specific law or political convention, are nothing but human beings. I can hardly imagine an attitude more dangerous, since we actually live in a world in which human beings as such have ceased to exist for quite a while; since society has discovered discrimination as the great social weapon by which one may kill men without any bloodshed; since passports or birth certificates, and sometimes even income tax receipts, are no longer formal papers but matters of social distinction. It is true that most of us depend entirely upon social standards; we lose confidence in ourselves if society does not approve us; we are—and always were—ready to pay any price in order to be accepted by society. But it is equally true that the very few among us who have tried to get along without all these tricks and jokes of adjustment and assimilation have paid a much higher price than they could afford: they jeopardized the few chances even outlaws are given in a topsy-turvy world.

The attitude of these few whom, following Bernard Lazare, one may call "conscious pariahs," can as little be explained by recent events alone as the attitude of our Mr. Cohn who tried by every means to become an upstart. Both are sons of the nineteenth century which, not knowing legal or political outlaws, knew only too well social pariahs and their counterpart, social parvenus. Modern Jewish history, having started with court Jews and continuing with Jewish millionaires and philanthropists, is apt to forget about this other trend of Jewish tradition—the tradition of Heine, Rahel Varnhagen, Sholom Aleichem, of Bernard Lazare, Franz Kafka or even Charlie Chaplin. It is the tradition of a minority of Jews who have not wanted to become upstarts, who preferred the status of "conscious pariah." All vaunted Jewish qualities—the "Jewish heart," humanity, humor, disinterested intelligence — are pariah qualities. All Jewish shortcomings— tactlessness, political stupidity, inferiority complexes and money-grubbing—are characteristic of upstarts. There have always been Jews who did not think it worth while to change their humane attitude and their natural insight into reality for the narrowness of caste spirit or the essential unreality of financial transactions.

History has forced the status of outlaws upon both, upon pariahs and parvenus alike. The latter have not yet accepted the great wisdom of Balzac's *"On ne parvient pas deux fois"*; thus they don't understand the wild dreams of the former and feel humiliated in sharing their fate. Those few refugees who insist upon telling the truth, even to the point of "indecency," get in exchange for their unpopularity one priceless advantage: history is no longer a closed book to them and politics is no longer the privilege of Gentiles. They know that the outlawing of the Jewish people in Europe has been followed closely by the outlawing of most European nations. Refugees driven from country to country represent the vanguard of their peoples—if they keep their identity. For the first time Jewish history is not separate but tied up with that of all other nations. The comity of European peoples went to pieces when, and because, it allowed its weakest member to be excluded and persecuted.

manifesta° Coffee Break

liverpool biennial

'We Refugees' by Hannah Arendt reprinted by permission of Harcourt, Inc. First published in *The Menorah Journal* (New York), 1 (1943).

'Beyond Human Rights' by Giorgio Agamben reprinted by permission of University of Minnesota Press. From *Means without End: Notes on Politics*, translated by Vincenzo Binetti and Cesare Casarino, University of Minnesota Press, 2000, pp. 15–26. Originally published as *Mezzi senza fine*, Bollati Boringhieri editori s.r.l., 1996.

'An Incomplete Manifesto for Growth' by Bruce Mau reprinted by permission of Bruce Mau Design, Inc.

Editor: Paul Domela
Contributing editor: Hedwig Fijen
Production editor: Helen Tookey
Discussion editor: Jonathan Turner
Design: Alan Ward @ axisgraphicdesign.co.uk
Cover image by LOVE Creative
Paper cover: 300gsm matt coated woodfree
Paper inside: 140gsm Planoplus
Typefaces: Lucida and Lucida Sans
Printing: Editoriale Bortolazzi Stei, Verona

Published by Liverpool Biennial of Contemporary Art Ltd.
ISBN 0-9536761-6-1

Coffee Break is a cooperative initiative by the International Foundation Manifesta (IFM) in Amsterdam and Liverpool Biennial. Coffee Break is part of a large Network Programme 2002–2005 in which the IFM is creating a platform for research and critical reflection.

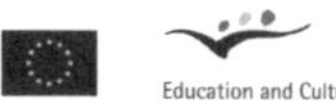
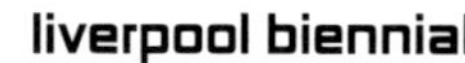
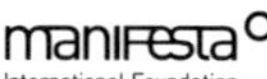

Education and Culture

Culture 2000

liverpool biennial

maniFesta°
International Foundation

Contents

Foreword
Lewis Biggs

The International Foundation Manifesta was founded to support artists through sharing information and creating networks of art advocates. The biennial nomadic Manifesta exhibition was the spoon that stirred the pot. The context of its creation in the mid-1990s was specific: a post-Cold War Europe in which the softening rigidities of the previous decades needed re-shaping. To my mind, Manifesta was intended – explicitly or not – to heal a wound in Europe's culture.

Within the UK, one effect of the events of 1989 was to direct attention to the continuing political/economic/social divisions exacerbated by the Thatcher years: the 'North–South divide'. The potential for rethinking East–West ruptures in Europe was paralleled in England by the opportunity to re-address North–South fractures. Manifesta 3, in Ljubljana in 2000, focused on a seamless Europe. The first Liverpool Biennial, in 1999, held the promise of an England constructed in a different way. ('Borders' was the theme of Manifesta 3, 'global traces' that of the Liverpool show.)

When Henry Meyric Hughes suggested that Liverpool Biennial become a partner in creating a 'New Manifesta Network', Paul Domela and I were delighted to agree. Thank you Henry and the Board, Hedwig and all at Manifesta.

Manifesta embraces internationalism and change through 'show and tell' – the moving spotlight of its exhibition. Liverpool Biennial embeds internationalism and change by reaching always deeper into the social and physical fabric of one city. By sharing experiences, learning and celebrating the differences between all the organisations in the Network, all the participants can enter a new space – an open, freer space – in which to consider afresh the role of the artist and art advocate.

Through three 'Coffee Breaks' in Liverpool, we found ourselves exploring ideas such as 'host', 'guest', 'feast', 'family', 'occupation' – the basic human facts that lie behind professional networking. We took time out exploring how to live creatively in a city – using the spaces between buildings, the gaps between organisational structures, seeing bombsites as new foundations, picking at the loose edges of the fabric. The lasting value of Coffee Break in Liverpool has not been print or even art, but the contact between people. Things happen between people when you rub them one against the other in a spirit of friendly criticality, always questioning and leaving traces of those questions: tea leaves and coffee grounds through which to imagine a future.

Manifesta Coffee Breaks in Liverpool
Hedwig Fijen

At the first Manifesta Coffee Break in Liverpool, which took place on 19–20 October 2002, Chris Dercon, a former board member of the Manifesta Foundation, acted as mediator for the two-day workshop. He invited one of the participants to comment on the concept behind the working methodology that had been previously discussed, as well as the consequences of such action in light of the idea of 'mediating the mediators and the mediation'. Dercon warned the auditorium that the findings might be distressing and even embarrassing for us, but that this was, supposedly, exactly why we were here at this Manifesta Coffee Break. He went on to say that at the end of the meeting we should respond to the unpleasant findings by tackling some of the urgent questions we had asked ourselves during the gathering.

This is an apt description of the significance of the Manifesta Coffee Breaks, which served to kick off a series of events in Liverpool, England, bringing together a unique group of art professionals from various generations, geopolitical backgrounds and levels of experience.

After producing three editions of Manifesta, the Foundation wanted to assemble its collective experiences through a more concrete concept and in a less orthodox setting. Former board member Hans Ulrich Obrist considered the idea of not simply organising a traditional conference programme but rather concentrating entirely on a feature common to all conferences, namely, the coffee-and-tea break, as a way for Manifesta to reflect on the logistics of updating its parameters and redirecting its strategies.

Manifesta has always been regarded as a lucid and flexible mobile structure continually in the process of transforming itself – as something diverse and heterogeneous, essentially open and willing to integrate and make connections with various initiatives. With this in mind, a summer school, or think-tank, was launched in the early years of the new millennium, to allow ourselves a kind of free-standing time-out from the usual institutional routines – a retreat, as it were, or interactive workshop, in which we could consider, in closed sessions and with a more informal and open discussion, the repositioning of contemporary art practices. These gatherings are merely one form of an ongoing dialogue between artists, theoreticians and everybody else.

The Manifesta Coffee Breaks provide a connection with Manifesta, and not only with the European biennial exhibition but also with those collaborations that have, ever since its inception, been constantly developing around the biennial and among all the individuals who have ever been involved with it. The first steps were taken soon after the close of Manifesta 3, held in Ljubljana, Slovenia, in 2000, when the Manifesta Foundation initiated a framework for preserving its memory. The re-launching of our Manifesta Network Programme allowed us to turn a large-scale event into a more diverse project through which a theoretical substructure was now able to support those concerns suggested by the exhibitions, thus opening new doors into the domain of contemporary art. With a generous grant from the European Commission Culture 2000 programme, we were able to inaugurate the first series of three Coffee Breaks.

At various meetings around Europe, we have discussed whether we should provide broader access to the knowledge we have accumulated over the years. Our knowledge, however, is not merely digital; it also involves such practical matters as introducing one person to another and providing a hands-on approach to methods for creating new projects.

As always, there are more questions than answers. Our burgeoning archives, which exist alongside the biennial exhibitions, currently play the role of 'spirit-keeper' for Manifesta. Should the archives (documents pertaining to the memory of previous shows) travel from one host city to the next? And, crucially, what is the difference between the 'off-show' (research and archival material) and the 'show-off' (the Manifesta exhibitions themselves)?[1] One particular line of thought, admittedly radical for an art biennial, suggests that, in the future, curatorial teams might wish to be completely liberated from the task of physically organising an exhibition.

The Manifesta Coffee Breaks are only part of a larger series of structural activities, initiated in 2002 by the International Foundation Manifesta, that aim specifically at a critical analysis and discussion of Manifesta's position, while formally establishing the organisation as a multifunctional platform for information and exchange. Our goal was to utilise the 'passive paper archive' as a way of turning the information we had accumulated into a proactive resource. This overall programme of activities focuses primarily on the development of mediating tools that provide stronger links to audiences. It includes publicly accessible databases, artists' archives (both digital and analogue), seminars such as the Manifesta Coffee Breaks, meetings and discussions, presentations and screenings, such as the *Decoding Europe* series, and publications, such as the *Manifesta Journal* – all of which seek to involve a broad audience in the activities of Manifesta while opening up critical debate surrounding its functions. These activities are not organised solely by Manifesta, but are co-produced by (or commissioned by) external partners throughout Europe. After all, the original parameters and structures are there to be reinvented.

The International Foundation Manifesta, based in Amsterdam, and the Liverpool Biennial, as represented by Lewis Biggs and Paul Domela, worked together as collaborative partners on the three editions of the Coffee Breaks hosted in 2003 and 2004, with the event hosts providing superb hospitality. On behalf of all participants in the Manifesta Coffee Breaks, I would like to thank all our Liverpool colleagues for their tireless support and commitment in this project; we look forward to strengthening our relationships with them in the near future.

Notes

1. To quote Chris Dercon, the mediator of the first Coffee Break in Liverpool.

Everything But the Coffee...
Paul Domela

In his Nexus lecture 'The Idea of Europe' George Steiner identifies the coffee house or café as one of the foundations of Europe: a public meeting space, open to all for reflection or conspiracy. This not only brings to mind the Central European tradition of the polyglot intellectual, of which Steiner himself is a notable example, but it also recalls images of the exile, the émigré, the refugee: Lenin drinking coffee in the Café Odeon, Kandinsky inventing *Der Blaue Reiter* over coffee in Sindelsdorf, Joyce's *Finnegans Wake*. Habermas noted the central role of coffee houses in the formation of a public sphere in eighteenth-century London, spawning a multifarious legacy, from the *Guardian* to Lloyd's of London.

Manifesta Coffee Break charts three meetings hosted by Liverpool Biennial and International Foundation Manifesta between 2002 and 2004 around visual art and contemporary curatorial work in a changing Europe. The title 'Coffee Break' refers to the idea that the most inspiring observations usually happen in between disciplines, positions, papers or presentations. The three weekends in Liverpool provided a stimulant for knowledge exchange, debate, discussion and chat between artists, curators and other cultural producers living in and/or working in and around Europe.

Manifesta was the first biennial exhibition to explicitly address the European context following Europe's own, more liberating, 9/11 – the fall of the Berlin Wall in 1989. fifteen years later, ten countries of the former East acceded to the European Union, but not on equal terms. Increasingly, migration not only to but also within Europe is selectively denied, and the idea of a multicultural society appears abandoned. Political discussion has become dominated by emotionalised debates on limits to tolerance, enforced assimilation, re-awakened nationalisms and religious fundamentalisms. In a European project predicated on economic integration, it is exceedingly urgent to counter these reactionary populisms with renewed investment in cultural dialogue, not as objective but deliberately as 'means without end'.

You will find in this publication texts and shards of discussions around three pressing notions: the refugee, hospitality and occupation. In raising these notions, it was not and is not our intention to ascribe to artists or cultural producers a special responsibility (beyond that which we all share as citizens or denizens) to act – to produce meaning – politically. An awareness of cultural heterogeneity in Europe displaces the dominance of questioning representational conventions, locked in a closed system of cultural values and meaning, in favour of an emerging, dialogical process of knowledge production – a political project as much as a praxis of plurality. The process of negotiating shared space turns our attention to the sociality of art-making, shifting the emphasis from an instantaneous to a durational concept of the aesthetic, from a specular to a more collaborative encounter with the art process – all the while aware of the disciplinary dimension of art and culture. The way these developments affect artists and curators provided the context for our discussions and gave impetus to critical reformulations of the Manifesta project in particular.

We chose to open this publication with 'We Refugees', a text published by Hannah Arendt in 1943. 'We Refugees' analyses the refugee condition of a persecuted people and reminds us not only that 'refugees represent the vanguard of their peoples', but also that 'the comity of Europe fell apart the moment it excluded its weakest members'. The text is the basis for Giorgio Agamben's essay 'Beyond Human Rights' and we thought it interesting to reproduce them here together. Arendt's text is as relevant as ever. Most will say that the project Europe succeeds in order not to repeat, but increasingly we see with Agamben how the state of exception is re-emerging, perpetuating what cannot be repeated in different names and places.

The publication is organised chronologically, with observations from the discussions accompanying the essayistic contributions, but inevitably misses out the invaluable gossip, gestures and asides of a true coffee break. Rather than giving you the semblance of completeness, we chose to select those writerly bits and pieces that rise and fall in the course of conversation – intentionally leaving out the quiet doldrums and unintentionally the passages garbled by the microphone. Before each section you will find the email invitation setting out the parameters of each Coffee Break. This gives you an idea of the questions we posed ourselves at the outset and provides a compass by which to gauge our thoughts. I hope you find something of value and perhaps an inducement for further conversation – in Liverpool, in Nicosia, or some place unintended.

Refugee

From:
Date:
To:
Subject:

Dear

The Manifesta network is growing, entering a new phase, with projects expanding our means of
thinking exhibitions and opening onto different conceptions of place. For some time we have
been talking about the need to set time aside in this transition and discuss the relation between
Manifesta and our evolving practices in a radically crystallising political climate.

In conversations with many of you in Frankfurt, the most pressing issue that emerged was the
populist wave of demands for restrictions on migration and the pressures toward managing
cultural difference. It is clear that these developments impact across the political spectrum
affecting resources and perceptions open to artists' practices and experimentation.

In thinking about these issues should we begin to see Manifesta as a refugee exhibition,
following Hannah Arendt's 'the true avant-garde is the refugee'? And how could we begin to
understand Negri and Hardt's reconceptualised 'multitude' in the specificity of our different
practices as artists, directors, writers or curators in translating performing networks?

We would like to open a moment for reflection and debate around these themes, avoiding the
formal arrangements of a summer school, conferences, workshops and so on. In a retreat from
existing processes and models we aim for the intensity of invention. Between the speeds of
expectation and immediate public scrutiny we propose to script this time COFFEE BREAK.

COFFEE BREAK takes place from Saturday and Sunday the 19th and 20th of October. Hosted by
Liverpool Biennial and chaired by Chris Dercon, we envisage an afternoon, evening and morning
for you and all the partners of the Manifesta network to talk to each other – *off the record*.

On a practical level we are able to offer you expenses for travel up to €300 (exceptions
accepted) and hotel accommodation in Liverpool for two nights. Please contact me before August
23rd to arrange your booking.

Attached to this email you will find the three texts that will inform our discussions. We ask you
to read these texts and the selected reviews on Manifesta 1-4 which will be send seperately to
your postal address. We very much look forward to seeing you in Liverpool.

Yours sincerely,

Paul Domela

Coffee Break Steering Group: Lewis Biggs (Liverpool Biennial), Chris Dercon (ex-board member,
IFM), Paul Domela (Liverpool Biennial), Colin Fallows (Head of Research, Liverpool School of Art
and Design), Hedwig Fijen (secretary-general, IFM), Christoph Grunenberg (Tate Liverpool), Henry
Meyric Hughes (president, IFM), Hans Ulrich Obrist (ex-board member, IFM)

Beyond Human Rights
Giorgio Agamben

In 1943, Hannah Arendt published an article titled 'We Refugees' in a small English-language Jewish publication, the *Menorah Journal*. At the end of this brief but significant piece of writing, after having polemically sketched the portrait of Mr Cohn, the assimilated Jew who, after having been 150 per cent German, 150 per cent Viennese, 150 per cent French, must bitterly realise in the end that 'on ne parvient pas deux fois', she turns the condition of countryless refugee – a condition she herself was living – upside down in order to present it as the paradigm of a new historical consciousness. The refugees who have lost all rights and who, however, no longer want to be assimilated at all costs in a new national identity, but want instead to contemplate lucidly their condition, receive in exchange for assured unpopularity a priceless advantage: 'History is no longer a closed book to them and politics is no longer the privilege of Gentiles. They know that the outlawing of the Jewish people of Europe has been followed closely by the outlawing of most European nations. Refugees driven from country to country represent the vanguard of their peoples.'[1]

One ought to reflect on the meaning of this analysis, which after fifty years has lost none of its relevance. It is not only the case that the problem presents itself inside and outside of Europe with just as much urgency as then. It is also the case that, given the by now unstoppable decline of the nation-state and the general corrosion of traditional political-juridical categories, the refugee is perhaps the only thinkable figure for the people of our time and the only category in which one may see today – at least until the process of dissolution of the nation-state and of its sovereignty has achieved full completion – the forms and limits of a coming political community. It is even possible that, if we want to be equal to the absolutely new tasks ahead, we will have to abandon decidedly, without reservation, the fundamental concepts through which we have so far represented the subjects of the political (Man, the Citizen and its rights, but also the sovereign people, the worker, and so forth) and build our political philosophy anew starting from the one and only figure of the refugee

The first appearance of refugees as a mass phenomenon took place at the end of World War I, when the fall of the Russian, Austro-Hungarian and Ottoman empires, along with the new order created by the peace treaties, upset profoundly the demographic and territorial constitution of Central Eastern Europe. In a short period, 1.5 million White Russians, seven hundred thousand Armenians, five hundred thousand Bulgarians, a million Greeks, and hundreds of thousands of Germans, Hungarians, and Romanians left their countries. To these moving masses, one needs to add the explosive situation determined by the fact that about 30 per cent of the population in the new states created by the peace treaties on the model of the nation-state (Yugoslavia and Czechoslovakia, for example) was constituted by minorities that had to be safeguarded by a series of international treaties – the so-called Minority Treaties – which very often were not enforced. A few years later, the racial laws in Germany and the civil war in Spain dispersed throughout Europe a new and important contingent of refugees.

We are used to distinguishing between refugees and stateless people, but this distinction was not then as simple as it may seem at first glance, nor is it even today. From the beginning, many refugees, who were not technically stateless, preferred to become such rather than return to their country. (This was the case with the Polish and Romanian Jews who were in France or Germany at the end of the war, and today it is the case with those who are politically persecuted or for whom returning to their countries would mean putting their own survival at risk.) On the other hand, Russian, Armenian and Hungarian refugees were promptly denationalised by the new Turkish and Soviet governments. It is important to note how, starting with World War I, many European states began to pass laws allowing the denaturalisation and denationalisation of their own citizens: France was first, in 1915, with regard to naturalised citizens of 'enemy origin'; in 1922, Belgium followed this example by revoking the naturalisation of those citizens who had committed 'anti-national' acts during the war; in 1926, the Italian Fascist regime passed an analogous law with regard to citizens who had shown themselves 'undeserving of Italian citizenship'; in 1933, it was Austria's turn; and so on, until in 1935 the Nuremberg Laws divided German citizens into citizens with full rights and citizens without political rights. Such laws – and the mass statelessness resulting from them – mark a decisive turn in the life of the modern nation-state as well as its definitive emancipation from naïve notions of the citizen and a people.

This is not the place to retrace the history of the various international organisations through which single states, the League of Nations and, later, the United Nations have tried to face the refugee problem, from the Nansen Bureau for the Russian and Armenian refugees (1921) to the High Commission for Refugees from Germany (1936) to the Intergovernmental Committee for Refugees (1938) to the UN's International Refugee Organisation (1946) to the present Office of the High Commissioner for Refugees (1951), whose activity, according to its statute, does not have a political character but rather only a 'social and humanitarian' one. What is essential is that each and every time refugees no longer represent individual cases but rather a mass phenomenon (as was the case between the two World Wars and is now once again), these organisations as well as the single states – all the solemn evocations of the inalienable rights of human beings notwithstanding – have proved to be absolutely incapable not only of solving the problem but also of facing it in an adequate manner. The whole question, therefore, was handed over to humanitarian organisations and to the police.

The reasons for such impotence lie not only in the selfishness and blindness of bureaucratic apparatuses, but also in the very ambiguity of the fundamental notions regulating the inscription of the native (that is, of life) in the juridical order of the nation-state. Hannah Arendt titled the chapter of her book *Imperialism* that concerns the refugee problem 'The Decline of the Nation-State and the End of the Rights of Man'.[2] One should try to take seriously this formulation, which indissolubly links the fate of the Rights of Man with the fate of the modern nation-state in such a way that the waning of the latter necessarily implies the obsolescence of the former. Here the paradox is that precisely the figure that should have embodied human rights more than any other – namely, the refugee – marked instead the radical crisis of the concept. The conception of human rights based on the supposed existence of a human being as such, Arendt tells us, proves to be untenable as soon as those who profess it find themselves confronted for the first time with people who have really lost every quality and every specific relation except for the pure fact of being human.[3] In the system of the nation-state, so-called sacred and inalienable human rights are revealed to be without any protection precisely when it is no longer possible to conceive of them as rights of the citizens of a state. This is implicit, after all, in the ambiguity of the very title of the 1789 *Déclaration des droits de l'homme et du citoyen*, in which it is unclear whether the two terms are to name two distinct realities or whether they are to form, instead, a hendiadys in which the first term is actually always already contained in the second.

That there is no autonomous space in the political order of the nation-state for something like the pure human in itself is evident at the very least from the fact that, even in the best of cases, the status of refugee has always been considered a temporary condition that ought to lead either to naturalisation or to repatriation. A stable statute for the human in itself is inconceivable in the law of the nation-state.

It is time to cease to look at all the declarations of rights from 1789 to the present day as proclamations of eternal metajuridical values aimed at binding the legislator to the respect of such values; it is time, rather, to understand them according to their real function in the modern state. Human rights, in fact, represent first of all the originary figure for the inscription of natural naked life in the political-juridical order of the nation-state. Naked life (the human being), which in antiquity belonged to God and in the classical world was clearly distinct (as *zoë*) from political life (*bios*), comes to the forefront in the management of the state and becomes, so to speak, its earthly foundation. Nation-state means a state that makes nativity or birth (*nascita*) (that is, naked human life) the foundation of its own sovereignty. This is the meaning (and it is not even a hidden one) of the first three articles of the 1789 Declaration: it is only because this declaration inscribed (in articles 1 and 2) the native element in the heart of any political organisation that it can firmly bind (in article 3) the principle of sovereignty to the nation (in conformity with its etymon, native [*natío*] originally meant simply 'birth' [*nascita*]). The fiction that is implicit here is that *birth* (*nascita*) comes into being immediately as *nation*, so that there may not be any difference between the two moments. Rights, in other words, are attributed to the human being only to the degree to which he or she is the immediately vanishing presupposition (and, in fact, the presupposition that must never come to light as such) of the citizen.

If the refugee represents such a disquieting element in the order of the nation-state, this is so primarily because, by breaking the identity between the human and the citizen and that between nativity and nationality, it brings the originary fiction of sovereignty to crisis. Single exceptions to such a principle, of course, have always existed. What is new in our time is that growing sections of humankind are no longer representable inside the nation-state – and this novelty threatens the very foundations of the latter. Inasmuch as the refugee, an apparently marginal figure, unhinges the old trinity of state-nation-territory, it deserves instead to be regarded as the central figure of our political history. We should not forget that the first camps were built in Europe as spaces for controlling refugees, and that the succession of internment camps–concentration camps–extermination camps represents a perfectly real filiation. One of the few rules the Nazis constantly obeyed throughout the course of the 'final solution' was that Jews and Gypsies could be sent to extermination camps only after having been fully denationalised (that is, after they had been stripped of even that second-class citizenship to which they had been relegated after the Nuremberg Laws). When their rights are no longer the rights of the citizen, that is when human beings are truly sacred, in the sense that this term used to have in the Roman law of the archaic period: doomed to death.

The concept of refugee must be resolutely separated from the concept of the 'human rights', and the right of asylum (which in any case is by now in the process of being drastically restricted in the legislation of the European states) must no longer be considered as the conceptual category in which to inscribe the phenomenon of refugees. (One needs only to look at Agnes Heller's recent *Theses on the Right of Asylum* to realise that this cannot but lead today to awkward confusions.) The refugee should be considered for what it is, namely, nothing less than a limit-concept that at once brings a radical crisis to the principles of the nation-state and clears the way for a renewal of categories that can no longer be delayed.

Meanwhile, in fact, the phenomenon of so-called illegal immigration into the countries of the European Union has reached (and will increasingly reach in the coming years, given the estimated twenty million migrants from Central European countries) characteristics and proportions such that this reversal of perspective is fully justified. What industrialised countries face today is a permanently resident mass of non-citizens who do not want to be and cannot be either naturalised or repatriated. These non-citizens often have nationalities of origin, but, inasmuch as they prefer not to benefit from their own states' protection, they find themselves, as refugees, in a condition of de facto statelessness. Tomas Hammar has created the neologism of 'denizens' for these non-citizen residents, a neologism that has the merit of showing how the concept of 'citizen' is no longer adequate for describing the social-political reality of modern states.[4] On the other hand, the citizens of advanced industrial states (in the United States as well as Europe) demonstrate, through an increasing desertion of the codified instances of political participation, an evident propensity to turn into denizens, into non-citizen permanent residents, so that citizens and denizens – at least in certain social strata – are entering an area of potential indistinction. In a parallel way, xenophobic reactions and defensive mobilisations are on the rise, in conformity with the well-known principle according to which substantial assimilation in the presence of formal differences exacerbates hatred and intolerance.

Before extermination camps are reopened in Europe (something that is already starting to happen), it is necessary that the nation-states find the courage to question the very principle of the inscription of nativity as well as the trinity of state-nation-territory that is founded on that principle. It is not easy to indicate right now the ways in which all this may concretely happen. One of the options taken into consideration for solving the problem of Jerusalem is that it become – simultaneously and without any territorial partition – the capital of two different states. The paradoxical condition of reciprocal extraterritoriality (or, better yet, aterritoriality) that would thus be implied could be generalised as a model of new international relations. Instead of two national states separated by uncertain and threatening boundaries, it might be possible to imagine two political communities insisting on the same region and in a condition of exodus from each other – communities that would articulate each other via a series of reciprocal extraterritorialities in which the guiding concept would no longer be the *ius* (right) of the citizen but rather the *refugium* (refuge) of the singular. In an analogous way, we could conceive of Europe not as an impossible 'Europe of the nations', whose catastrophe one can already foresee in the short run, but rather as an aterritorial or extraterritorial space in which all the (citizen and non-citizen) residents of the European states would be in a position of exodus or refuge; the status of European would then mean the being-in-exodus of the citizen (a condition that obviously could also be one of immobility). European space would thus mark an irreducible difference between birth (*nascita*) and nation in which the old concept of people (which, as is well known, is always a minority) could again find a political meaning, thus decidedly opposing itself to the concept of nation (which has so far unduly usurped it).

This space would coincide neither with any of the homogeneous national territories nor with their *topographical* sum, but would rather act on them by articulating and perforating them *topologically* as in the Klein bottle or in the Möbius strip, where exterior and interior in-determine each other. In this new space, European cities would rediscover their ancient vocation of cities of the world by entering into a relation of reciprocal extraterritoriality.

As I write this essay, 425 Palestinians expelled by the state of Israel find themselves in a sort of no-man's-land. These men certainly constitute, according to Hannah Arendt's suggestion, 'the vanguard of their people'. But that is so not necessarily or not merely in the sense that they might form the originary nucleus of a future national state, or in the sense that they might solve the Palestinian question in a way just as insufficient as the way in which Israel has solved the Jewish question. Rather, the no-man's-land in which they are refugees has already started from this very moment to act back onto the territory of the state of Israel by perforating it and altering it in such a way that the image of that snowy mountain has become more internal to it than any other region of Eretz Israel. Only in a world in which the spaces of states have been thus perforated and topologically deformed and in which the citizen has been able to recognise the refugee that he or she is – only in such a world is the political survival of humankind today thinkable.

(1993)

Notes

1. Hannah Arendt, 'We Refugees', *Menorah Journal*, no. 1 (1943), p. 77.

2. Hannah Arendt, *Imperialism*, Part II of *The Origins of Totalitarianism*, New York: Harcourt, Brace, 1951, pp. 266-98.

3. Arendt, *Imperialism*, pp. 290-95.

4. Tomas Hammar, *Democracy and the Nation State: Aliens, Denizens, and Citizens in a World of International Migration*, Brookfield, Vt.: Gower, 1990.

An Incomplete Manifesto for Growth*
Bruce Mau

1.   **Allow events to change you**. You have to be willing to grow. Growth is different from something that happens to you. You produce it. You live it. The prerequisites for growth: the openness to experience events and the willingness to be changed by them.

2.   **Forget about good**. Good is a known quantity. Good is what we all agree on. Growth is not necessarily good. Growth is an exploration of unlit recesses that may or may not yield to our research. As long as you stick to good you'll never have real growth.

3.   **Process is more important than outcome**. When the outcome drives the process we will only ever go to where we've already been. If process drives outcome we may not know where we're going, but we will know we want to be there.

4.   **Love your experiments (as you would an ugly child)**. Joy is the engine of growth. Exploit the liberty in casting your work as beautiful experiments, iterations, attempts, trials, and errors. Take the long view and allow yourself the fun of failure every day.

5.   **Go deep**. The deeper you go the more likely you will discover something of value.

6.   **Capture accidents**. The wrong answer is
the right answer in search of a different question.
Collect wrong answers as part of the process.
Ask different questions.

7.   **Study**. A studio is a place of study. Use the
necessity of production as an excuse to study.
Everyone will benefit.

8.   **Drift**. Allow yourself to wander aimlessly.
Explore adjacencies. Lack judgment. Postpone
criticism.

9.   **Begin anywhere**. John Cage tells us that not
knowing where to begin is a common form of
paralysis. His advice: begin anywhere.

10. **Everyone is a leader**. Growth happens.
Whenever it does, allow it to emerge. Learn to
follow when it makes sense. Let anyone lead.

11. **Harvest ideas**. Edit applications. Ideas need a
dynamic, fluid, generous environment to sustain
life. Applications, on the other hand, benefit from
critical rigour. Produce a high ratio of ideas to
applications.

12. **Keep moving**. The market and its operations
have a tendency to reinforce success. Resist it.
Allow failure and migration to be part of your
practice.

13. **Slow down**. Desynchronise from standard time
frames and surprising opportunities may present
themselves.

14. **Don't be cool**. Cool is conservative fear dressed in black. Free yourself from limits of this sort.

15. **Ask stupid questions**. Growth is fuelled by desire and innocence. Assess the answer, not the question. Imagine learning throughout your life at the rate of an infant.

16. **Collaborate**. The space between people working together is filled with conflict, friction, strife, exhilaration, delight, and vast creative potential.

17. **----------**. Intentionally left blank. Allow space for the ideas you haven't had yet, and for the ideas of others.

18. **Stay up late**. Strange things happen when you've gone too far, been up too long, worked too hard, and you're separated from the rest of the world.

19. **Work the metaphor**. Every object has the capacity to stand for something other than what is apparent. Work on what it stands for.

20. **Be careful to take risks**. Time is genetic. Today is the child of yesterday and the parent of tomorrow. The work you produce today will create your future.

21. **Repeat yourself**. If you like it, do it again. If you don't like it, do it again.

22. **Make your own tools**. Hybridise your tools in order to build unique things. Even simple tools that are your own can yield entirely new avenues of exploration. Remember, tools amplify our capacities, so even a small tool can make a big difference.

23. **Stand on someone's shoulders**. You can travel farther carried on the accomplishments of those who came before you. And the view is so much better.

24. **Avoid software**. The problem with software is that everyone has it.

25. **Don't clean your desk**. You might find something in the morning that you can't see tonight.

26. **Don't enter awards competitions**. Just don't. It's not good for you.

27. **Read only left-hand pages**. Marshall McLuhan did this. By decreasing the amount of information, we leave room for what he called our 'noodle'.

28. **Make new words**. Expand the lexicon.
The new conditions demand a new way of thinking.
The thinking demands new forms of expression.
The expression generates new conditions.

29. **Think with your mind**. Forget technology. Creativity is not device-dependent.

30. **Organisation = Liberty**. Real innovation in design, or any other field, happens in context. That context is usually some form of cooperatively managed enterprise. Frank Gehry, for instance, is only able to realise Bilbao because his studio can deliver it on budget. The myth of a split between 'creatives' and 'suits' is what Leonard Cohen calls a 'charming artefact of the past'.

31. **Don't borrow money**. Once again, Frank Gehry's advice. By maintaining financial control, we maintain creative control. It's not exactly rocket science, but it's surprising how hard it is to maintain this discipline, and how many have failed.

32. **Listen carefully**. Every collaborator who enters our orbit brings with him or her a world more strange and complex than any we could ever hope to imagine. By listening to the details and the subtlety of their needs, desires, or ambitions, we fold their world onto our own. Neither party will ever be the same.

33. **Take field trips**. The bandwidth of the world is greater than that of your TV set, or the Internet, or even a totally immersive, interactive, dynamically rendered, object-oriented, real-time, computer graphic simulated environment.

34. **Make mistakes faster**. This isn't my idea – I borrowed it. I think it belongs to Andy Grove.

35. **Imitate**. Don't be shy about it. Try to get as close as you can. You'll never get all the way, and the separation might be truly remarkable. We have only to look to Richard Hamilton and his version of Marcel Duchamp's large glass to see how rich, discredited, and under-used imitation is as a technique.

36. **Scat**. When you forget the words, do what Ella
did: make up something else... but not words.

37. **Break it, stretch it, bend it, crush it,
crack it, fold it**.

38. **Explore the other edge**. Great liberty exists
when we avoid trying to run with the technological
pack. We can't find the leading edge because it's
trampled underfoot. Try using old-tech equipment
made obsolete by an economic cycle but still rich
with potential.

39. **Coffee breaks, cab rides, green rooms**.
Real growth often happens outside of where we
intend it to, in the interstitial spaces – what Dr
Seuss calls 'the waiting place'. Hans Ulrich Obrist
once organised a science and art conference with all
of the infrastructure of a conference – the parties,
chats, lunches, airport arrivals – but with no actual
conference. Apparently it was hugely successful
and spawned many ongoing collaborations.

40. **Avoid fields**. Jump fences. Disciplinary
boundaries and regulatory regimes are attempts to
control the wilding of creative life. They are often
understandable efforts to order what are manifold,
complex, evolutionary processes. Our job is to jump
the fences and cross the fields.

41. **Laugh**. People visiting the studio often
comment on how much we laugh. Since I've become
aware of this, I use it as a barometer of how
comfortably we are expressing ourselves.

42. **Remember**. Growth is only possible as a product of history. Without memory, innovation is merely novelty. History gives growth a direction. But a memory is never perfect. Every memory is a degraded or composite image of a previous moment or event. That's what makes us aware of its quality as a past and not a present. It means that every memory is new, a partial construct different from its source, and, as such, a potential for growth itself.

43. **Power to the people**. Play can only happen when people feel they have control over their lives. We can't be free agents if we're not free.

* Written in 1998, the *Incomplete Manifesto* is an articulation of statements that exemplify Bruce Mau's beliefs, motivations and strategies. It also articulates how the BMD studio works.

Is There a Mediator in the Empire?
Dieter Lesage
Translated by Chris Turner

The Multitude against Empire

Empire, the book by the Italian philosopher Antonio Negri and the American literary theorist Michael Hardt, aims to be both an analytical portrait of the political constitution of the present and a call to contest that new world order which the authors call 'Empire'.[1] The subject carrying out this desired contestation is given the name 'multitude'. On the one side, then, a political order, on the other the contesting of that order; on the one side Empire, on the other the multitude – this is in itself enough to suggest that, in the imperial context, a mediator is required. But mediation is precisely what *Empire* wants nothing of. Between Empire and the multitude, say the authors, there is no possible mediation:

> Imperial power can no longer resolve the conflict of social forces through mediatory schemata that displace the terms of conflict. The social conflicts that constitute the political confront one another directly, without mediations of any sort. This is the essential originality of the imperial situation. Empire creates a greater potential for revolution than did the modern regimes of power because it presents us, alongside the machine of command, with an alternative: the set of all the exploited and the subjugated, a multitude that is directly opposed to empire, with no mediation between them.[2]

Before we come to the question of how this thesis is to be understood and what the consequences of it might be for the position of the 'mediator' today, we shall first have to clarify the terms in play in this confrontation without possible mediation: namely, 'Empire' and 'multitude'. According to the definition of Negri and Hardt, Empire is the form the modern concept of sovereignty has assumed in the postmodern era of globalisation. At the supranational level, we see a process of constitutionalisation in which several institutions and organisations are articulated to one another. This overall constitutional framework might be conceived as a pyramidal structure, made up of three progressively expanding 'levels'. At the narrow tip of the pyramid we find the United States. It exercises military hegemony, is capable of acting alone, but prefers operations within a wider framework under the aegis of the United Nations. At this first level of the global constitutional pyramid we also find other nation states, which together control the financial instruments and which are grouped in a number of organisations such as the G7. Also on this first level are a certain number of financial and military organisations, such as the International Monetary Fund, the World Bank, the World Trade Organization and NATO. On the second level of the pyramid of the global constitution, Negri and Hardt put the transnational corporations and the other nation states. Lastly, the third level is said to be made up of organisations that are supposed to represent populations. Apart from the United Nations we find here the media, the major religious organisations and the non-governmental organisations (NGOs). Each in its way makes a claim, or aspires, to represent 'the people' on a global scale. For Negri and Hardt, this tripartite division of the constitution of the contemporary global order constitutes an argument for naming that order *imperial.* This is because this type of tripartite division is also found in Polybius, in his apologetic description of the Roman Empire. According to Polybius, the Roman Empire combines the so-called 'good' forms of government in a perfect balance: the Emperor represents monarchy, the Senate represents aristocracy, the *comitia* represent democracy. The imperial constitution in which these institutions maintain an equilibrium prevents monarchy from becoming a tyranny, aristocracy from becoming an oligarchy and democracy from collapsing into anarchy. A partisan of contemporary Empire could also describe it in Polybian terms as a functional equilibrium between the monarchist military hegemony of the USA, the aristocratic influence of the transnational corporations and of a small club of nation states and, lastly, the contemporary *comitia* in the form of the other nation states and their representation in the United Nations, the NGOs and the media etc. Defenders of Empire could recognise in this tripartite constitutional division a form of proto-federalism of checks and balances at the global level, in which several institutions exert mutual restraint on one another and balance each other out. By contrast, the authors of *Empire* call for resistance against this constitutionalisation of the imperial world order. Political philosophy, which regards it as imperative in this age of globalisation to rethink the role of the transnational institutions, stands in their view in a political tradition that is 'corrupt' in one precise sense: that it persists in conceiving politics as an authoritarian instance that is alone capable of transcending the violence and chaos of the multitude. According to Negri in his book *Kairos, Alma Venus, Multitudo: nove lezioni impartite a me stesso,* we should free ourselves from the concept of sovereignty which is the original sin of political philosophy.[3] In his view, this concept has never been anything but a strategy for confiscating the power of the multitude. In *Empire*, Negri and Hardt demonstrate how the concept of sovereignty, which they reject, is closely linked to the concept of mediation.

Modern Metaphysics and Mediation

For Negri and Hardt, mediation constitutes the very heart of the modern political philosophy of sovereignty. In the history of modern philosophy, the concept of mediation is a counter-revolutionary concept that serves only to confiscate the constituent power of the multitude. In the century/ies of the Enlightenment, say Negri and Hardt, the major philosophical programme consisted in setting in place a 'transcendental apparatus capable of disciplining a multitude of formally free subjects'.[4]

> It was paramount to avoid the multitude's being understood, à la Spinoza, in a direct, immediate relation with divinity and nature, as the ethical product of life and the world. On the contrary, in every case mediation had to be imposed on the complexity of human relations. Philosophers disputed where this mediation was situated and what metaphysical level it occupied, but it was fundamental that in some way it be defined as an ineluctable condition of all human action, art, and association.[5]

In keeping with this transcendental logic, the triad *vis–cupiditas–amor*, which constituted the matrix of revolutionary thought, had to be replaced by a triad of specific mediations.

> Nature and experience are unrecognizable except through *the filter of phenomena*; human knowledge cannot be achieved except through *the reflection of the intellect*; and the ethical world is incommunicable except through the *schematism of reason*. What is at play is a form of mediation, or really a reflexive folding back and a sort of weak transcendence, which relativizes experience and abolishes every instance of the immediate and absolute in human life and history.[6]

According to Negri and Hardt, the strategic importance of this triple schema of mediations was to prevent the multitude discovering itself as the power that constituted reality through its direct capacity to will, to desire and to love. Negri and Hardt show how the history of modern metaphysics, from Descartes to Hegel, can be read as the history of a transcendental vampirism that removes any life and dynamism from being. To speak of philosophical vampires is to put it too weakly. Following Schopenhauer, Negri and Hardt denounce Hegel as an 'intellectual Caliban', after the character in Shakespeare's *Tempest*, and they remind us of the irony of that particular figure becoming emblematic of resistance to any form of Western hegemony in the post-colonial studies they hold dear.

This apparatus of mediations put in place by an entire metaphysical tradition of modernity – though Negri and Hardt insist it was only one of the two traditions of modernity and that there was another tradition, a revolutionary one, that led from Machiavelli via Spinoza to Marx – finds its political counterpart in a whole tradition within modern political philosophy that has applied itself to dominating the revolutionary potential of the multitude by setting in place a transcendent political apparatus. It was by evoking the danger of a war of each against all that Thomas Hobbes believed he had demonstrated the need for a sovereign who would guarantee order and peace. In Hobbes the multitude which, left to its own devices, would perish in chaotic disorder, must necessarily become a people, if only because individuals have in common the will to survive.

Which brings us to the question of how precisely to define that other key concept in *Empire*: namely, the multitude. The concept seems to function in *Empire* a little like a proper name, the proper name of a collective entity, of the presumed subject of anti-imperial resistance to which *Empire* is addressed as a manifesto. But who or what precisely is this 'multitude'?

In the history of philosophy, the concept of 'multitude' – as a translation of the Latin *multitudo* – has often been used as a mere synonym for the concept of 'people'. Machiavelli, for example, to whom Negri and Hardt frequently refer, makes no analytical distinction between the concepts *populo* and *moltitudine*. Now, from modern times onwards, the concept of 'people' has been developed in the way that is familiar to us, whilst the concept of 'multitude' has been reserved to indicate some particular crowd or mass of people, more or less fortuitously assembled, and disorganised. The concept of 'multitude' thus became a reference to the people in a pejorative way: that is to say, to the people at risk of descending into anarchy. Historically, *Empire* ascribes this distinction to Thomas Hobbes. Since Hobbes, the multitude has become a purely negative concept. Throughout the history of modern political philosophy, 'the multitude' refers generally – except, that is, in Spinoza – to the zero degree of collectivity. All this explains why the concept of multitude had until recently remained philosophically idle. And this rendered the vacant concept of interest to the new political theory of the collectivity that *Empire* seeks to be. *Empire* strives to conceive the multitude positively, but that effort, it must be said, is not always so convincing. One of the first 'definitions' of the concept we encounter, in a book in which the concept appears on almost every page, runs as follows: 'The multitude is a multiplicity, a plane of singularities, an open set of relations, which is not homogeneous or identical with itself and bears an indistinct, inclusive relation to those outside of it'.[7]

According to this definition, it is virtually impossible not to belong to the multitude. One cannot, indeed, fall outside of a collectivity, defined as a set of relations, if that set also has relations with those outside itself, and does so inclusively. Elsewhere Negri defines the multitude as 'a set of singularities, whose tool of survival is the brain and whose productive force is cooperation'.[8] For Negri, there is no longer any need for mediation, insofar as the pertinent question becomes that of knowing how this biopolitical mass can exercise a 'government of self', of which it is, in his view, absolutely capable. In what follows I should like to develop some thoughts on the role of 'mediators' in, and in relation to, Empire, and in, and in relation to, the multitude.

The General Mediator

Instead of saying that, in the Empire, there is no longer any mediation, it would be better to explain that there is, in the Empire, nothing but mediation and that it is precisely because of the generalisation of mediation that there is no longer any mediation. Paraphrasing a famous concept of Marx's, we might say that in Empire the 'general mediator' is actualising him/herself. To avoid a certain confusion, we should note that 'general mediator' is a type of certificate that can be obtained in some US universities – a certificate as a generalist mediator, by contrast with the family mediator – and that it is also the title of a master's degree one can obtain at some European universities. Now, none of these are my concern when I speak of the 'general mediator' in the context of the problematic of Empire. Let us say that the certificates and master's degrees in mediation that can be obtained in various places are merely concrete examples of what concerns me. One might say, in fact, that by a strange inversion, in the Empire, in which no mediation is said to be possible any longer, the mediator has become the emblematic figure *par excellence.* So central is the position of the mediator – if we can still speak in terms of centrality, in terms of centre and periphery – that one has almost lost count of the contexts in which 'mediators' are regarded as essential. The mediator as diplomat has, of course, been around for a long time, but diplomacy now seems to be the order of the day in many other contexts apart from international relations. Diplomacy has become fractal. There are mediators in local, regional, national and supranational administrations, serving as interfaces between citizens and administrators on the lines of the Swedish 'ombudsman', an office which dates back to 1809. There is the 'social mediator' who negotiates between the social partners to arrive at social accords or pacts; there is the 'penal mediator' who negotiates between offender and victim to achieve a form of reparation; there is the 'artistic mediator' who negotiates between sponsors and artists so that works are produced which meet the desires of both. There are mediators in schools, who act as an interface between students and teachers, mediators in problem neighbourhoods, mediators in the underground, mediators everywhere. It seems that, in some museums, which are not real museums, there are even mediators between the visitors and the art works.

Besides the professions which literally bear the name 'mediator', there are many others which are also, from the functional standpoint, forms of mediation. There are quite old professions that we can now see, ultimately, to be 'mediating' professions. For example, the neighbourhood policeman in the old Tintin comics has also become a 'mediator'. In the so-called 'problem' neighbourhoods in particular there are now any number of different types of 'mediators'. The neighbourhood policeman isn't the only one who has to manage mediation in his district: social workers, street youth workers and others all have mediatory responsibilities.

It is no surprise then that mediation is becoming a popular sport: American campuses have their 'campus mediation centres' and you can, for example, learn the principles of 'verbal judo' in them.

This fractalisation of mediation, both in the form of the creation of new occupations of mediator and of a redefinition of old occupations in terms of mediation, reflects a heightened regard for communication that is entirely characteristic of Empire. For example, the 'mediator in the museum' is clearly the product of a redefinition of the function of museum attendant. Now, what purpose does this redefinition of the museum attendant's function fulfil? It obliges the attendant, a creature of legendary taciturnity, to speak, to communicate. But that is not all. As the new-style attendant is supposed to speak with the visitor, this redefinition of the museum attendant's profession also obliges the visitor to speak at the same time. Even the art work is obliged to communicate. Communication has become a categorical imperative: thou shalt communicate.

The phenomenon of the museum attendant turned 'artistic mediator' seems equally interesting to me from another point of view. Without wishing to play the wicked philosopher in relation to this kind of initiative, which, in practice, may be entirely congenial, one might push the point further of what it means that it is a warden or attendant who has become a 'mediator'. We might ask ourselves, in particular, whether 'museum mediation' cannot be understood as the mutation of the agency which in the past guaranteed that the visitor conformed to the museum's disciplinary code into an agency of 'control' more concerned with shaping the visitor's subjectivity. A visit that respects the rules of bodily behaviour is no longer sufficient (not touching the exhibits, not speaking too loudly, not stealing); the aim is also to transform the visitor's soul. Might we not, then, regard this initiative, congenial as it may be, as exemplifying the transformation of the disciplinary society into a society of control, a transformation which Negri and Hardt, together with Deleuze and his particular reading of Foucault, see as constitutive of Empire?

If we come back now to the museum – or, rather, to the art centre, since the object is no longer the conservation of art works, but the creation of experiences – and to the so-called 'problem' areas of our cities and all the different types of mediators who come together there, a thought analogous to that inspired by the reconfigured museum attendant presses itself upon us. What the 'mediators' in the problem neighbourhoods do is shape subjectivities. It is no longer enough that all the inhabitants respect public property and keep the peace; we are interested now in people's most intimate attitudes towards each other. It is not enough for young people to leave the elderly alone; they are taken into the Old People's Homes and made to have coffee and biscuits with the residents, so that the two groups can get to know each other better. Clearly, once again, this may produce images that warm the cockles of one's heart, as the expression goes. Aziz and Mohamed chatting with grandma over a cup of tea: a really happy sight! (And, so as not to be suspected of expressing some partiality in my examples, I could also have said: Eli and Benjamin nibbling pretzels at grandma's – kosher pretzels!) But isn't there also a problematical side to this; isn't there at least an ambiguity to be pointed up, over and above the congenial feel of such initiatives? *Empire* describes the poor metropolitan neighbourhoods and the American 'inner cities' as the most fragile, fragilising places in the imperial order. Empire, we are told, does not have to fear a conflict between the First World and the Third World, so much as one between the inner-city districts of the First World. This is because these megalopolises are the sites of Empire where the socio-economic rifts are most visible, where the juxtapositions are most poignant. In spite of all the good work they do, and precisely through that work, the mediators in the poor neighbourhoods underwrite the status quo and reduce the potentialities for insurrection. Negri and Hardt would no doubt say that between the suburbs and the gated communities of Los Angeles, no mediation is possible any longer. It is clear now that this does not mean there is no longer any mediation in Empire. Far from it. Empire has pulled off the masterstroke that consists in rendering transcendence immanent, in internalising it. The eternal peace Empire seeks to establish, following the example of the Roman empire, is something it has fallen to the mediators to attempt to achieve in the poor neighbourhoods. Rather than believe in the neutrality of the mediators, we should consider them as subjective forces superadded to a social context in which these forces are supposed to sway the subjectivities involved in that context in some particular direction. At neighbourhood level, (imperial) peace is not an organisation of space so that bodies do not come into conflict, but a particular configuration productive of subjectivities.

Is There a Mediator in the Empire?

If we have been able to observe that there are mediators everywhere and that mediation is the most widespread of activities, where might the impression have come from today that it is, of all things, a mediator that Empire lacks? At this present moment – April 2002 – the Israeli–Palestinian conflict is at its height. A world full of mediators looks on, spurned. Some tell themselves that we are, in the end, all Palestinians. Others do not agree. But what is sure and certain is that we are all mediators! Is there really no one who can mediate in the Near East? The most revealing event in this whole drama was doubtless the siege of the Church of the Nativity in Bethlehem. At the very place where the Mediator of all mediators was said to have been born, there was a total blockade.[9] Even the Holy See, a mediator among the political authorities of this world if ever there was one, does not seem capable of achieving much. Two years after the papal visit to Bethlehem, which the Bethlehem 2000 project had renovated from top to bottom for the occasion of the Holy Year, the village is in ruins. But, some will say, we have had Colin Powell. And the question becomes one of whether Colin Powell could ever qualify as a 'mediator'. Now, we have seen to what extent the choice of Colin Powell as mediator had more to do with the relations of force underlying the conflict than the supposed neutrality of the mediator in question. We saw a real battle between aspiring mediators before Colin Powell came on the scene almost, as we might say, 'as the victor', even if, after all his travels, he has not managed to achieve his goal – which was perhaps precisely his goal after all. On the scene of international diplomacy the choice of a mediator mainly reflects hegemonies within the imperial order. *Empire* assumes that between the three layers of Empire there might be said to be a hybrid, but functional equilibrium. Now, at the level of the discussion regarding which mediators are to be sent into conflict situations, there turns out to be a struggle for hegemony, albeit a timid one, between the monarchical, aristocratic and democratic components of the imperial order.

The role of the mediator assumes a neutrality which, on account of the collapse of transcendence, no longer exists. That transcendence was precisely the guarantee of the possibility of a neutrality. Now, if there is no longer any neutrality, there cannot be any mediators either. Every mediator necessarily then becomes an impostor. It might be objected to this that, though there is no longer any neutrality, there are still in fact mediators. For there to be a mediator, it is not necessary that he or she should be neutral, but that he or she should be recognised as such by the parties involved. Not an essentialist neutrality, so to speak, but a functional neutrality is required for someone to be able to qualify as mediator. It will be increasingly difficult to find functional mediators. The mediator is understood as a force superadded to a geopolitical balance of forces to bring those relations into the desired imperial equilibrium.

The Spirit of Mediation

Given the range of mediators, it might have been useful to make a distinction between two types of mediation, even though such a typology would immediately be blurred by a number of hybrid types. By reference to the opposition developed in *Empire* between 'constituted power' and 'constituent power' as synonyms of Empire and the multitude, we might have spoken of 'constituted mediators' and 'constituent mediators'. The 'constituted mediator' would be the person who intervenes in a conflict or dispute with two or more parties that already stand in a certain relation to each other before the intervention of the mediator. The 'constituent mediator' would be the one who himself constitutes contacts between different parties. The 'constituent mediator' is the 'networker'. The aim of such a distinction might be to rescue the 'constituent mediator' from the suspicion that ultimately his work merely consolidated the equilibria of Empire. Unlike the work of the 'constituted mediator', which might be said to contribute to the imperial balance, the work of the 'constituent mediator' would be situated rather on the side of the multitude. To simplify things, one might ask oneself whether, from a contestatory standpoint, one should not then distinguish between the 'good' and the 'bad' mediator. To dramatise matters further, the question is whether, from an ontological standpoint, one should not have made a distinction between the mediator who corrupts and the mediator who generates. We shall see that this typology will be difficult to maintain. The mediator who intervenes in a conflict between parties can act in such a way that that conflictual relation is redefined in terms of collaboration. On the other hand, the networking mediator runs the risk of seeking, once cooperation has been established, to make him/herself useful in an artificial or manipulative way.

One might, in fact, wonder whether the profession of mediator today, that is to say, in a network society, should not provoke identity problems in those who identify themselves as 'mediators'. Far be it from me to seek to medicalise the mediator. On the other hand, it will be understood that what concerns me here is the problem that arises regarding the position of mediator as a specific professional figure in an occupational landscape in which every worker can be described as a mediator or, in other words, where mediation has no specific quality. We might take the following observation by Maurizio Lazzarato in this way:

> Twenty years of restructuring of the big factories has led to a curious paradox. The various different post-Fordist models have been constructed both on the defeat of the Fordist worker and on the recognition of the centrality of (an ever increasingly intellectualized) living labor within production. In today's large restructured company, a worker's work increasingly involves, at various levels, an ability to choose among different alternatives and thus a degree of responsibility regarding decision making. The concept of 'interface' used by communications sociologists provides a fair definition of the activities of this kind of worker – as an interface between different functions, between different working teams, between different levels of the hierarchy, and so forth.[10]

In the networks and, therefore, in contemporary work, all workers are mediators. Yet there are workers who call themselves 'mediators' who see their role as being to create networks. So what could explain the fact that, to paraphrase George Orwell's famous saying, 'All animals are mediators, but some animals are more mediators than others'? In a connectionist world that is internalising the spirit of mediation, how can 'mediators' continue to find legitimation? If connectionism becomes generalised and 'the general mediator' becomes a reality, there will be no need for 'mediators' any longer. Clearly, the mediator is aware of this. We may imagine a number of traps the mediator is in danger of falling into. In fact, the problem of the mediator as 'networker' is that, very often, at the point when the connection or the contact has been made, he or she has become superfluous. Mediators will be forced to find good reasons why it is necessary for them to remain involved in the cooperation they have set in train. The danger may be that the mediators, as specialists in connecting people, will focus all their efforts on the connection itself. It may, then, be that the project fails because communication between the persons involved is rendered difficult by the one who is, in fact, supposed to facilitate it. A mediator fails when the network he/she produces is conceived in such a way that it is obligatory to pass through the mediator. In this way, the constituent mediator, the networker, the producer of relations of cooperation and hence someone involved in ontological *generatio*, begins to regard him/herself as an institution and slides into ontological *corruptio*. Good mediators are generous mediators, so generous that they are prepared to disappear from the scene the moment they see that everything is sorting itself out. A good mediator is a mediator who disappears.

Notes

1. Michael Hardt and Antonio Negri, *Empire*, Cambridge, MA, and London: Harvard University Press, 2000.

2. Hardt and Negri, *Empire*, p. 393.

3. Roma: Manifestolibri, 2000. Quoted here from the French translation, *Kairos, Alma Venus, Multitude: Neuf leçons en forme d'exercice*, trans. Judith Revel, Paris: Calmann-Lévy, 2001, p. 148.

4. Hardt and Negri, *Empire*, p. 78.

5. Hardt and Negri, *Empire*, p. 78.

6. Hardt and Negri, *Empire*, pp. 78–79.

7. Hardt and Negri, *Empire*, p. 103.

8. Negri, *Kairos, Alma Venus, Multitude*, p. 147.

9. Within the Anglican tradition, there is 'the Church of the Mediator'. Jesus Christ is regarded as a 'mediator', the only one God sent down to earth. 'The Church of the Mediator' refers, for its vision, to the epistles of St Paul, particularly 1 Tim. 2:5-6a. It is interesting to see how 'the Church of the Mediator' has articulated its christology by making comparisons with the whole culture of 'easy' mediation.

10. Maurizio Lazzarato, 'Immaterial Labor', in Paolo Virno and Michael Hardt (eds), *Radical Thought in Italy: A Potential Politics*, Minneapolis and London: University of Minnesota Press, 1996, p. 134.

Discussion (raw extracts)

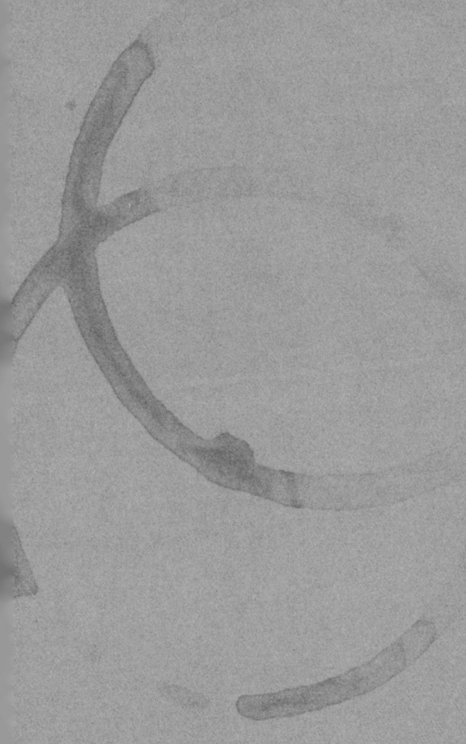

We tried to establish Manifesta as a kind of door opening up to eastern Europe, coming up with a new idea about the contemporary art scene in Europe, to give chances, to make people aware, to give a kind of new consciousness. Today, we are trying to redefine for ourselves what that means, curating in this European context. Do we still know what Europe is?

What to do in the light of expectations, in light of the former Manifesta histories, and what to do about the expectations of the Foundation itself, the Board, the local organisers and their dependency on the local funders. What is the power of the money brought in by the Foundation on the European level and the money brought in locally? What about the expectations of the curators and the artists?

The third aspect which struck me yesterday was a repeated call for investment in the local art scene.

the necessity to work on the whole idea of the time and timing of the event, the duration of Manifesta. The necessity to stress dialogue: events, exchange, instead of just an exhibition

Five, Manifesta is a brand; through its vast network, through its working methods, through its occupation of different European spaces

what does research mean for us?

Public intellectuals need a forum and Manifesta should become more of a forum to them.

the necessity of an archive

What does Manifesta really mean for the artist?

What does Manifesta mean for the development of art?

Manifesta wants to favour thinking space

critics are getting sceptical about the cultural
space of visual arts and what visual art can
bring to the cultural space

visual arts today are acting like a sponge,
soaking up architecture, design, and other
media

I prefer to look at art as yeast, a yeast that
breeds with other fields.

the countryless refugee as a paradigm for a
new historical consciousness

It is possible to seek in the text the conceptual
underpinnings of the architectonic language of
what Manifesta could be, of what it is not yet.
To provide a projection, a trajectory into
furthering a world in which the spaces of
states have been perforated and typologically
deformed.

non-place as the space of art

the space of flows as the new spatial logic that
may define the new international art world.

Many different modernities.

Refugees serve as an incursion into this unhinging
notion of 'citizen' and Manifesta in furthering
Europe may work within unravelling of this
deceit to imply the potential for human existence

I'm not sure if the nation state really declines
through migration.

The nomad is the one who doesn't care much
about nations.

being a nomad is a privilege

a wilful abandonment of citizenship and certain
rights

Wherever Manifesta goes it should be clear that this is a space with certain rights, in the ethical sense.

If you look at the precise terms of Agamben it might give a blueprint for a European thing called Manifesta.

I'm wondering if calling Manifesta nomadic is not an over-easy way to be on the side of the weak, the refugee, because I would ask whether Manifesta is not more like a transnational corporation

How much does the negotiation with the local authority determine the place for Manifesta?

Manifesta could go where it is not welcome

What is missing from the discussion is the aspect of artists

It is not a refugee or a nomad, it's a commuter.

The centrality of Manifesta not only causes a fall-out or a discussion amongst artists in the host city, it brings in incredibly decentralised artists from regions, it brings non-commercial artists into play.

It is important to start to get to know place early.

as an artistic community, knowing all our limits, why don't we take up other formats to operate in.

An exhibition is not a good format in which to take up that negotiation.

It is the first time we have admitted that Manifesta is a corporation and is a brand.

everybody should have the right to growth but also has the right to cultivate his own underdevelopment. Growth is not innocent.

process is as important as outcome

I strongly believe that art moves through metaphor.

San Sebastian should discuss politics but through metaphors. Only bad art has straight answers.

Manifesta needs new tools. Manifesta is more and we need to branch out. Corporate terminology has to be used in another direction. Somehow Manifesta manages to keep the team together. This meeting is a clear sign of something that doesn't happen for Documenta or Venice. In those cases the team leaves after the job. We stand on each other's shoulders.

On the one hand the potential of the metaphor and on the other hand the need to be transparent. Is opening archives a metaphor?

You have to start creating spaces with the audience. Allowing access is a top-down way of looking at it...

We are with Manifesta and the Liverpool Biennial in between these two worlds, the world which Agamben has described – not the world of the refugee, but his idea of theory as a gesture – and the ideas of Bruce Mau, the idea of the symbolical and the indexical, between the allegorical and whatever is there. It is a further complication of the problematic marriage of art and theory.

the buzzwords of the artistic critique of the sixties have been incorporated by new management. Authenticity, identity, invention. This is what corporate managers will be talking about. I think this means we have to redefine our critical position.

For instance the insistence on research

Research is a device to ask for time to do labour. Maybe we should think about what labour is. Anything can be labour. Everybody is a mediator. If curators claim to be mediators this is a claim that is not very grounded.

Labour today means making connections between people. Everybody is communicating. In this sense, everybody is always networking.

In the network everybody is a mediator.

Empire ends with two interesting demands. The demand of global citizenship, everybody should have the right to be where he wants to be. Secondly, everything can be qualified as labour – and, I should add, should be paid for it as well.

The problem is values.

But the point of business is different.

Why and who for? Who are we speaking to?
Sixty per cent of people living in England live
within 5 miles of where they were born.

An image for our network is the people who
spoke Latin in the Middle Ages, that ability to
speak across other cultures in the international
language of modern art. But that kind of
network has nothing to do with what people do
in their daily lives.

In Liverpool they are selling public space (my
space).

Doing art about these things is important and
has real impact.

What is it that we care about? What do we want
to change?

The most important issue was pointed out in
relation to the archive: not simply making it

accessible, but having the participation of the people who use it in creating the archive.

One of the most interesting things today are the changes from an audience as spectator to an audience as participant.

If the audience is seen as participant, the artist and curator have to open up to ideas which are not necessarily their own. There is a tremendous challenge for all of us to try to do that.

The audience becomes the heart of the working process. How do we see the audience?

Who is the Host?

From:
Date:
To:
Subject:

Dear

We would like to invite you to the second Liverpool Coffee Break on 20 and 21 February 2004. Coffee Break is organised by Liverpool Biennial in cooperation with International Foundation Manifesta to discuss questions of art and curatorial practice in a changing Europe.

In these debates the notions of hospitality, host and hosting have remained largely unexplored. What are the expectations of the host and what do we expect from the host; what can we ask for and what are our responsibilities? Where the traditional understanding of hospitality derives from the logic of exchange and gift, on the slippery slope of contemporary practice this logic now seems too neat.

In the words of Michel Serres, the field of the host is a dark puddle. 'In the logic of exchange, or really instead of it, it manages to hide who the receiver is and who the sender is, which one wants war and which one wants peace and offers asylum.' We propose to reflect on these questions from theoretical concepts to everyday issues of eating, drinking, and sleeping. What possibilities do we have in our practices between hosting and hosted, institutional interests and cultural tourism? If ethics is understood as the place where the familiar opens to the unfamiliar, we suggest hospitality as the act that marks that space. How do we rescue it within the increasingly xenophobic politics of citizenship?

Coffee Break takes place on Friday 20 and Saturday 21 February 2004. Chaired by Ole Bouman, the Friday programme will be open to the public and will inform a 'closed' round table session on Saturday. Along with yourself we have invited all partners in the Manifesta network and a small number of practitioners. The proceedings will be used as the basis for a publication to be published in spring 2005.

On a practical level we are able to offer you economy travel to and from Liverpool and hotel accommodation for two nights. Please contact   to confirm your participation and arrange your travel. To reduce the cost of airfare we recommend that you include a Saturday night in your stay.

We very much hope you are willing and able to accept our invitation and look forward to seeing you in Liverpool.

Yours sincerely,

Paul Domela

Coffee Break Steering Group: Ole Bouman (editor, *Archis*; curator, Manifesta 3), Paul Domela (Liverpool Biennial), Iara Boubnova (board member, IFM), Hedwig Fijen (secretary-general, IFM), Christoph Grunenberg (Tate Liverpool)

Coffee Break is a cooperative initiative by the International Foundation Manifesta (IFM) in Amsterdam, and Liverpool Biennial. Coffee Break is part of a large Network Programme 2002–2005 in which the IFM is creating a platform for research and critical reflection.

I give you a very warm welcome to the Tate Gallery Liverpool. My name is **Lewis Biggs**, and I'm the Chief Executive of the Liverpool Biennial. Since I've been in Liverpool now for fifteen or sixteen years, it falls to me to make the general welcome to you all. I'm thanking a number of people to start with. Because this is a coffee break, and because the point of a coffee break is to meet people and to talk, it's necessary to know at least some of the participants from the beginning. So, Paul Domela is the person who really has brought the programme of this coffee break together. The Tate is, of course, our host today, and Christoph Grunenberg is the Director. There's a fabulous Mike Kelley exhibition next door through this wall here, which opened last night.

We are basically here as guests of the International Foundation Manifesta. Henry Meyric Hughes, the president, is here, as is Hedwig Fijen, the founding director, and Marieke van Hal, the managing editor of the *Manifesta Journal*. And the reason the Tate, Liverpool Biennial and Manifesta are all here together is because the Biennial is a part of Manifesta's 'New Network Programme', which was set up a little more than a year ago to involve a number of organisations around Europe, alongside the main Manifesta event, which is a nomadic biennial.

Now I will introduce **Ole Bouman**, who will be the moderator for this afternoon. He is the editor of *Archis*, and was one of the curators for Manifesta 3 in Ljubljana. It falls to me to make a sad apology for **Nicolas Bourriaud**. He called this morning to say that his minister for culture has decided to make a lightning visit to the Palais de Tokyo this afternoon, and he has to be there with his minister. However, we have his text, and we haven't drawn lots yet, but someone is going to read or should I should say 'perform' the text. So, over to you **Ole**, thank you...

Thank you Lewis. It's good to be in Liverpool for a very interesting occasion. It's called a coffee break, although the setting is quite formal: you are there and I'm here. In a couple of minutes two other speakers will stand here addressing you. I, in the capacity of moderator, will try to produce a real debate, to go beyond the unilateral discourse into a real coffee break kind of conversation atmosphere.

Anyway, I would like to say a few words on the notion of hospitality, and the reason this should be discussed today in culture. I am from Holland, based in Amsterdam. It's the capital of a country which in these past couple of weeks has become known as hostile, not very hospitable to foreigners. Recently, our government decided to send away, or to deport, 26,000 asylum seekers to their 'home' states. But as we all know, many asylum seekers do not have the right papers. They may say they come from a certain state, but in the end, it's almost an arbitrary decision as to where they will be sent. Even their children, raised in Holland and sometimes not even speaking the languages of their parents, will be sent back to their home countries. This is a new step in Europe. I think many other countries are discussing this way to rid themselves of their problem with asylum seekers in one stroke, to send away thousands and thousands of people. So, discussing the notion of hospitality within this kind of cultural, political context is truly urgent.

If you think, for instance, about the ongoing discussion about art as a form of social engagement, vis à vis *art as an autonomous activity*, you will end up discussing notions of hospitality as well, because if you try to be a social activist through art you need a host, you need an audience, you need a context which can be defined as hosting. If you deny that host, if you are reluctant to engage with that host, then you might simply be fond of the autonomy of art. The same kind of relationship can be seen in terms of the debate about the 'white cube' versus site-specific art. Without making it explicit, you can see many references to the notion of hospitality. Is the 'white cube' a hospitable environment for art, or is it hostile? Is someone who provides the artist with a white cube, let's say a curator or museum director, a hospitable person or is he merely a lazy, passive, background figure who gives the artist the floor to do the work, to dance for the public? Even if you think of larger cultural or political debates, such as globalisation versus the local, you see this notion of hospitality in the way that people negotiate.

For Manifesta, this is the second time it has addressed the notion of hospitality. A couple of months ago in Amsterdam there was a series of presentations made by people involved in hosting, curating, art-producing or exhibition-producing, trying to figure out what was the productivity of a debate about hospitality. But the problem with that discussion in Amsterdam was that, by the end of the day, people became almost cynical. At the end, reluctantly, people found the courage to say that even if art shows, curators and artists do need a host, or a host city, or a host institution, you could always clearly define the special interest of each host in hosting that event. Pointing at the self-interest of the host to organise or enable art to exist might be an interesting observation, but it won't help us to dig into the productivity and the cultural relevance of hospitality as a positive cultural notion. Beyond that obvious self-interest, there might be something we can define which could go beyond facilitation, which is in itself a kind of productive contribution to the cultural production.

To summarise the debate, I would like to briefly sketch the benefits of hosting in the right way. If you are a guest, you may think of the host as the one who enables you to do things, who provides you with new contexts, who facilitates things for you, who provides you with an audience, and who gives you acknowledgment. So there are very positive notions related to hospitality. And also for the host, of course, there are many benefits. The guest is refreshing, gives you new insights, entertains you, maybe even gives you prestige, and helps you to expand your network. But if you think about these benefits, and if you think about the substance of the mutual benefits, it's mainly

Exotic Hospitality in the Land of Tolerance
Irina Aristarkhova

Prologue

One of my relatives (let's call him Ivan) was sent to the war in Chechnya during his military service. His unit was abducted and there was a suspicion that they had been 'sold' by one of their own men. They were beaten up and split into smaller groups. The Chechen abductors 'sold' him, or, probably, passed him as a 'gift' to an old couple living in a remote village. Ivan did various manual jobs and was treated well. Once, while working in the field, he decided to leave. He was not sure where to go, so he just walked towards the mountains. He encountered a Chechen man. The man was happy to meet a Russian soldier as he hoped to sell him, or so he said. Ivan did not care, since he was tired and just wanted to rest and to eat. While having a meal in the Chechen man's house, they chatted (after all, Russian is the *lingua franca* in the former USSR). They discovered that both had a younger sister. After feeding Ivan, his host/owner brought him to a visible footpath and said: 'Just follow this road all the way, it leads to Dagestan, out of here.' And they parted. Ivan was walking for a long time, and then he saw an old man on a donkey crossing the road. It was Dagestan. The Dagestani man asked him: 'Where would you like me to take you?' Ivan replied: 'To a police post.' There he was immediately put on a train with other Russians who were discharged and coming back home. He made a friend on the train and brought him to his house near Moscow for a meal, before his friend left for Siberia. Ivan is now married and has a child.

Europe and Hospitality

Immanuel Kant, who is usually credited with the elaboration of the modern Western conception of ethics and morality, judged nations according to their hospitality: the way they treated strangers in their lands. In his *Anthropology from a Pragmatic Point of View*[1] (a lecture from the 1770s, published posthumously) Kant formulated his opinion on 'The Character of the Nations'. From this text it becomes clear that he was probably rare among philosophers in the European tradition in being preoccupied with hospitality as a concept worth thinking through (albeit in a limited manner compared to his development of other concepts) and even worth using to judge national character. Elsewhere Kant clearly criticises the European inability to treat guests with hospitality, and European abuse of the hospitality of others in colonised lands.[2] However, what is more important for us here is that Kant positioned hospitality as a universal criterion for judgment of national character, though his own view of hospitality remained, problematically, the 'true' measurement.

According to Kant, the Germans are the most hospitable nation (it's not clear whether this means the most hospitable in Europe, or in the world), defined by the way they relate to strangers, and they have – as a result of that? – the best national character: 'The Germans are more hospitable to strangers than any other nation'.[3] The national character of the French is also defined by their relation to foreigners. Unlike the Germans, whose main national trait is 'good character', Kant states that the French are a 'courteous nation', especially to strangers, and they are also 'curious' about others – something that becomes a crucial point in

Derrida's analysis of hospitality: the desire for the Other and his or her difference. For Kant, this curiosity comes from the 'femininity' of the French nobility, who partake in a so-called lady-like way of speaking and behaving: 'the language of ladies has become the language shared by all high society. It cannot be disputed at all that an inclination of such a nature must also have influence on the ready willingness in rendering services, helpful benevolence, and the gradual development of human kindness according to principles'.[4] Derrida went even further to claim that hospitality is feminine par excellence, as I have discussed critically elsewhere.[5] To simplify somewhat the words of Kant, we conclude that the French are kind to foreigners because they use 'ladies' language', which makes them, supposedly, want to serve and please. This connection between hospitality and women is lost when one considers the matters of peace and war in Kant and further in Derrida.

With regard to the English people, Kant applies a notion rare in Western philosophy: he judges national character through *kindness.* The English, according to Kant, are not only inhospitable to strangers, but even to their own people, as a result of a fundamental lack of kindness compared to the French:

> The English people has a character ... that is more directly contrasted to that of the French people than to any other, because it renounces all kindness to others and even to people of their own; while kindness has been the most prominent social quality of the French. The English merely claim respect for themselves, so that, by the way, everybody can live according to his own will. For his own countrymen the Englishman establishes great benevolent institutions unheard of among all other peoples. But the foreigner who has been driven to England's shores by fate, and has fallen into dire need, will be left to die on the dunghill because he is not an Englishman, that is, not a human being.[6]

It is possible to argue that Kant's views of national characteristics are rather marginal to his overall corpus of works, especially as they were based on secondary sources and friends' opinions (after all, Kant never travelled). However, Kant himself did not seem to consider these notes marginal: this was almost the last text he prepared for publication before his death. It shows that the elderly Kant did not consider this lecture from the 1770s ungrounded and unimportant: on the contrary, he revisited it at the end of his life. Therefore, we might state with at least some certainty that Kant indeed prioritised the ethics of host–guest relations. This European philosopher, who is often heralded as the original reference point for European thought on hospitality, considered national character through a focus on nations' treatment of strangers, foreigners, and their own people.

What is hospitality then as defined by Kant? He did not provide a detailed account. His treatment of hospitality was mostly abstract and sketchy. He did not specify whether it entails bodily behaviour, the hosting of a guest in one's home, giving shelter, food, or special treatment compared to that normally given to family members. Kant did not elaborate a particular scenario of hospitality: what kind of situation may occur and how one should act. To put it simply, the question is whether it is enough to open the door and provide a glass of water to a thirsty stranger who asks for it – or does hospitality mean a smile, a welcoming to one's home, and an offer before a request is made or even conceived?

Here is the primary Kantian definition, an often cited passage taken from the text 'To Perpetual Peace': '[H]ospitality signifies the claim of a stranger entering foreign territory to be treated by its owner without hostility'. Both Levinas and Derrida take this definition further, and position hospitality as a much more radical notion that includes not only treatment of the Other without hostility, but a gesture of welcome, a smile, in addition to providing him with a refuge in the time of need. Derrida cites the European tradition of 'cities of refuge', and relates it to modern France.[7] Levinas discusses it in terms of Jewish history in times of persecution, war and exile.[8] Both of them go back to the primary texts of the Talmud, the Koran and the Bible as the sources for founding stories of hospitality.

Founding Stories of Hospitality

At the end of one of his texts on hospitality, Derrida recites two 'founding scene[s] of Abrahamesque hospitality', one from Genesis, and another one from Judges. In the second story the master of the house went out to people who wanted to 'penetrate' his pilgrim-guest, and told them:

> 'No, my brothers; I implore you, do not commit this crime. This man has become my guest; do not commit such an infamy. Here is my daughter; she is a virgin; I will give her to you. Possess her, do what you please with her, but do not commit such an infamy against this man.' The men would not listen to him. So the Levite took his concubine and brought her out to them. They had intercourse with her and outraged her all night till morning; when dawn was breaking they let her go.

> At daybreak the girl came and fell on the threshold of her husband's host, and she stayed there till it was full day. In the morning her husband got up and opened the door of the house. … [He] picked up his knife, took hold of his concubine, and limb by limb cut her into twelve pieces; then he sent her all through the land of Israel. He instructed his messengers as follows, 'This is what you are to say to all the Israelites, "Has any man seen such a thing from the day Israelites came out of the land of Egypt, until this very day? Ponder on this, discuss it; then give your verdict."' And all who saw it declared, 'Never has such a thing been done or been seen since the Israelites came out of the land of Egypt.'[9]

At the very end Derrida asks: 'Are we the heirs to this tradition of hospitality? Up to what point? Where should we place the invariant, if it is one, across this logic and these narratives? They testify without end in our memory.'[10]

Here we come across a situation of refusal of hospitality: the host protected his guest at the expense of his woman. She served the role of a substitute or a sacrifice – the notion that Derrida writes on extensively, when analysing hospitality. In that sense, this is not unconditional hospitality – what is asked for is not really provided. What is given out is a substitute. To give out a concubine, a wife or a daughter is to refuse unconditional hospitality, to be a bad host, ultimately. Or is it? It was refused to those who wanted to harm the guest, thus jeopardising the law of hospitality. This situation is not at all abstract for Levinas and Derrida, who both refer it to the Holocaust. European hosts of various nations had the choice of either extending their hospitality to the Jews, communists, Gypsies, and so on – and probably risking their own lives – or abandoning hospitality, leading to the assured suffering and probable death of their guests. Derrida recollects how France disowned its Jewish citizens of Algeria by taking their citizenship away during the Second World War.[11] This was done voluntarily, without Germany asking for it. The relation between host and guest is still one of the most politicised and complicated relationships, today in particular for immigrant 'guests'.[12]

In order to look at stories that consider the whole range of unconditional hospitality, we now turn to an example from a non-Abrahamic culture. For Vedic tradition, hospitality is not a marginal concern or an underground practice, but is central to the formation of culture as a whole. In her excellent work *Sacrificed Wife/Sacrificer's Wife: Women, Ritual and Hospitality in Ancient India* (1995) Stephanie Jamison carefully traces one particular detail of the complex role that hospitality plays in Indian tradition, specifically Vedic texts.[13] It is directly related to 'cultures of hospitality'. According to Jamison, hospitality is not simply an abstract concept, it is one of the central themes of Sanskrit culture, elaborated and developed: 'Hospitality, the appropriate behavior between host and guest, is a theme that infuses Sanskrit literature and as cultural behavior remains crucial to the present day. The duties of a host are set forth quite extensively in the official dharma and grhya manuals, and this codification of hostly behavior can be traced back to earlier texts... It is also a constantly recurring motif in literary texts in Sanskrit and other Indic languages.'[14]

I would like to present here some situations, discussed by Jamison, which can arise from what Derrida would call 'unconditional hospitality'. Ultimately, in these stories we encounter a localised and non-generalised hospitality, which is always both central to community and excessive, as a norm.

In a founding story of Indian culture the first man Manu is asked by two guests to give away his wife in order to perform a (hospitality) ritual. When he is ready to give her away to be sacrificed, the god Indra appears and tells him to perform the ritual with his two guests instead (as a punishment for demanding his wife, presumably). When Manu hesitates to kill two guests, Indra replies: 'A lord of guests [host] is master of his guests'.[15] Thus Manu's wife is set free. Another version of this story sees the wife actually killed. Jamison explains: 'Manu surrenders his possessions and his wife to strangers because of his obligations to *hospitality* and to the exchange relations on which hospitality depends. The source of the strangers' power and their loss of power is the same: the ambiguous and dangerous qualities intrinsic to the roles of both host and guest. This story expresses succinctly the real *anxieties of hospitality* that must have accompanied the inherited and dharmically enjoined host–guest relation.'[16]

Thus, the anxiety of hospitality, as Jamison calls it, is constitutive of the relations between host and guest. It is played out every time guests enter the house, or another 'hospitality situation' occurs. Here woman, just as in the Biblical story, embodies the symbolic nature of hospitality, and her role, though central, is based on her sacrifice. The importance of offering food at any cost, as a matter constitutive of 'pure hospitality' as a centre of community, is presented with utmost clarity and enacted in various scenarios in Vedic literature. One example tells us a fable of a fowler who captures a pigeon. Her pigeon husband is devastated but she insists that he welcome the fowler and ask him the question that sets hospitality in motion: What can I do for you? Though this now sounds to us ironically more appropriate for a situation within a 'hospitality industry', the question is an embodiment of hospitality. It signifies the vulnerability of the guest and the responsibility of the host, and vice versa. In the fable, the pigeon then attempts to supply the fowler's needs. He first makes a fire as a protection from the cold, but when the fowler asks for food, the pigeon must make the humiliating admission that he has none. After some thought and preparation, he ceremonially enters the fire himself, to make of himself the cooked food he needs to offer the fowler. 'Hospitality can hardly exact any higher price than self-immolation.'[17]

The question is how far one should go to practise hospitality, and what price hospitality should exact. This fable presents the scenario of Derrida's unconditional hospitality elaborated upon in detail, graphically: the price is anything. Anything should be provided for a guest, otherwise it is not pure hospitality. Hospitality demands everything, or it is not hospitality. This is the point of anxiety: the question 'What can I do for you?' can be read as meaning 'I would do anything for you, o guest'. Though it is a test of faith too, it is much more a test of hospitality as ethics of everyday life and relations with others.

Another story comes directly to the point of what unconditional hospitality entails, without compromise or substitute:

> A Brahman comes to Sibi in search of food and orders Sibi to prepare, cook, and serve his son Brhadgarbha as his meal. He agrees and sets about doing it, while the Brahman occupies the preparation time by burning down Sibi's house and its outbuildings. When Sibi finally catches up with him, Sibi merely says: 'Your food is ready, sir'. But the Brahman refuses it and orders Sibi to eat instead – in other words to eat his own son, whom he has already cooked for the Brahman's meal. Even then Sibi begins to comply, but the Brahman finally relents, snatches

his hand away, and restores the son to life. Again it is Sibi's lack of anger and willingness to obey that impress and please the Brahman.[18]

In Vedic tradition hospitality is assumed to be a practice of everyday life of a 'good' member of the community. The relation is not so much sacrificial and religious, since one can never be sure who the guest is. The tradition elaborates various details of what pure hospitality means, and what limitations one needs to be aware of. Again it is important to stress that in both traditions, Abrahamic as well as Vedic, women usually play the role of mediating objects, and rarely appear as receivers of hospitality. It is as though the traditions would crumble if women stopped playing their symbolic roles.

It seems that hospitality is not about generosity but rather scarcity. One receives the most praise when one is hospitable not because of one's wealth or ability, but despite one's inability and poverty. Hospitality is born out of constraint, and not as a result of abundance and excess. Therefore, hospitality should be found independent of one's means, whether financial, in terms of property, or otherwise. Pure hospitality in Indian culture means to put oneself at risk, to put oneself in a difficult situation – to the point of absurdity, from a 'reasonable' point of view. Otherwise it should be normal – to help, welcome, support, give. The position of the guest is precarious too. One should avoid asking for too much, one tries not to inconvenience one's host. But the guest should also allow the host to be hospitable, should allow his or her hospitality. Certainly, hospitality in the Indian tradition is not a matter of individual decision, it is a matter of community and relations within the community. To reiterate once again: hospitality is central to the formation and operation of Indian communities, both through the founding texts and through its integration into everyday life.

Tolerance and Hospitality

After examining Indian tradition and the cultural role of hospitality in the Indian context, we might notice that the Kantian definition of hospitality differs radically from the stories detailed above, both Vedic and Abrahamic. For Kant, universal hospitality is a matter of not being hostile to one's guest, provided the guest follows the rules of 'good behaviour'. The guest can then hope to receive a 'right of temporary visitation' (what today is known to us as a *visa*?). Derrida, though beginning with the Kantian definition, is also dissatisfied with it, especially in its application to the two main 'Others' of contemporary European culture: the Jew and the immigrant. The turn to hospitality is presented as a result of the urgent need to respond to what is happening in Europe, as revealed in the expression 'Fortress Europe'. Tolerance is seen as no longer sufficient, or even as hypocritical. The relation between the two concepts, 'tolerance' and 'hospitality', is not a simple matter of philosophical or political preference. Both have a history and both are part of a particular cultural concern. It would be correct to assume that if

European culture is dissatisfied with the concept and practice of 'tolerance', it is because it has a long tradition of it, and relation to it. It is dissatisfied with its own tradition of treating 'Others' with tolerance. Discussions on assimilation and on the extent to which immigrant 'guests' should follow their host country's customs seem to be an extension of the European culture of tolerance and its measure. The question is what the guest should do to be tolerated and, possibly, accepted as one of 'us'. Since it has been practised and elaborated within legal and political discourses, tolerance has become a culturally recognised concept. Explaining why tolerance is not a sufficient concept for Derrida, Giovanna Borradori argues:

> Derrida's treatment of hospitality comes straight from Kant. Hospitality is a more compassionate, and ultimately effective, alternative to tolerance. Tolerance is according to Derrida a paternalistic concept irremediably tainted by religious, and specifically Christian, implications developed in the Europe of the 1500s. For him, tolerance is a less neutral moral and political concept than it makes itself out to be. Also, he is bothered by the lack of authentic openness to the other that tolerance entails; the phrase 'threshold of tolerance,' which was used in France to indicate the limit beyond which it was no longer decent to ask a national community to welcome any more foreigners and immigrants, reveals this problematic implication.[19]

One might question whether Derrida's notion of hospitality comes directly from Kant (after all, I have tried to show here that the Kantian notion of hospitality is very limited); indeed, Derrida saw in hospitality a deconstructive potential. However, it is tolerance, and not hospitality, which is institutionalised in European societies. Hospitality is a much more unusual concept in Europe. A question we are likely to hear is 'How much longer can we tolerate this situation with immigrants?'; the issue of the limits of tolerance is being used in political campaigns across Europe.

It is problematic to appropriate hospitality as 'one's own' on the basis of its universality. That is why I would disagree profoundly with Derrida when he says that '[not] only is there a culture of hospitality, but there is no culture that is not also a culture of hospitality. All cultures compete in this regard and present themselves as more hospitable than the others. Hospitality – this is culture itself.'[20] The phrase 'every culture is a culture of hospitality' can also be read as an appropriation of hospitality, through the implication that *my* culture is a culture of hospitality. This seems problematic particularly in relation to those cultures that have championed other ways of relating to their guests – such as the concept of tolerance.

To summarise:

1. When we appropriate a concept of hospitality as ours, when we write about European hospitality no matter how critical we are, just because 'every culture

is a culture of hospitality', we violate important historical, philosophical and cultural differences.

2. After examining the Indian, non-Abrahamic tradition, it becomes clearer that hospitality is an underdeveloped concept in European thought, a marginal concern. Foundational texts in Vedic philosophy are preoccupied with the guest–host relationship, its anxieties, 'extremes' and frameworks. Those scenarios are far from the Kantian idea of the temporary visitor. They can help us further inform the scenarios of 'unconditional hospitality' offered by Derrida.

3. Neither the Abrahamic, the Indian, nor the recent European definitions of hospitality include women within host–guest relations on a symbolic or religious level; rather they position them as mediators or silent providers of 'femininity', of the feeling of 'being at home with oneself'.

4. Finally, European tradition developed a discourse of tolerance, which subsequently spread to other Western countries and is most commonly expressed in the idea of tolerating the differences of guests and immigrants through some unifying basis. This basis usually takes the form of the 'European values' of democracy, fraternity, freedom, equality, and – tolerance. One cannot simply replace tolerance with hospitality, because the former has a much richer meaning both socially and institutionally within Europe. The history of tolerance needs to be examined more carefully while we move towards desiring hospitality – to make sure that one does not collapse into the other, just as it is problematic to conflate cultures of hospitality with cultures of tolerance.

Epilogue

No need for stories, poems and myths that might shock European readers by their 'exotic hospitality' of eating sons, cooking oneself, or being hospitable to one's murderers. Ivan was at war, and he went to kill people – this is why soldiers are sent to war. Two people saved his life, by offering him food, shelter and direction, though they could well have used their host status in the opposite way. Ivan is alive today because of unconditional hospitality. 'Chechens are people. Dagestanis are people. We are bastards.' That is all he has to say today 'on the character of the nations'.

Notes

1. Immanuel Kant, *Anthropology from a Pragmatic Point of View*, trans. with an introduction and notes by Mary J. Gregor, The Hague: Nijhoff, 1974.

2. See Immanuel Kant, 'To Perpetual Peace: A Philosophical Sketch' (1795), trans. Ted Humphrey, Hackett Publishing, 2003, available at http://www.mtholyoke.edu/acad/intrel/kant/kant1.htm.

3. Kant, *Anthropology*, pp. 233–34. It is noteworthy that, according to a recent EU report, in the last two decades Germany has taken the highest number of immigrants per capita of any EU nation,

followed by the UK. Source: European Commission, *European Social Statistics: Migration*, Luxembourg: Office for the Official Publications of European Communities, 2002.

4. Kant, *Anthropology*, p. 228.

5. See I. Aristarkhova, 'Hospitality – Chora – Matrix – Cyberspace', *Filozofski Vestnik*, special issue, *The Body* (guest editor: Marina Grzinic Mauhler), 23.2 (2002), pp. 27–42.

6. Kant, *Anthropology*, p. 230.

7. See Jacques Derrida, *Adieu to Emmanuel Levinas*, trans. Pascale-Anne Brault and Michael Naas, Stanford: Stanford University Press, 1999; Jacques Derrida and Anne Dufourmantelle, *Of Hospitality: Anne Dufourmantelle Invites Jacques Derrida to Respond*, trans. Rachel Bowlby, Stanford: Stanford University Press, 2000; Jacques Derrida, *Acts of Religion*, ed. and with an introduction by Gil Anidjar, New York and London: Routledge, 2002.

8. See Emmanuel Levinas, *Totality and Infinity: An Essay on Exteriority*, trans. Alphonso Lingis, The Hague: Nijhoff, 2002 (1961).

9. Judges 19:23-30, cited in Derrida and Dufourmantelle, *Of Hospitality*, pp. 153–54.

10. Derrida and Dufourmantelle, *Of Hospitality*, p. 154.

11. See Derrida and Dufourmantelle, *Of Hospitality*, p. 143; and Derrida, *Adieu to Emmanuel Levinas*.

12. See the excellent book on this topic by Mireille Rosello, *Postcolonial Hospitality: The Immigrant as Guest*, Stanford: Stanford University Press, 2001.

13. See Stephanie Jamison, *Sacrificed Wife/Sacrificer's Wife: Women, Ritual and Hospitality in Ancient India*, Oxford: Oxford University Press, 1995.

14. Jamison, *Sacrificed Wife/Sacrificer's Wife*, p. 157.

15. Jamison, *Sacrificed Wife/Sacrificer's Wife*, pp. 22–23.

16. Jamison, *Sacrificed Wife/Sacrificer's Wife*, p. 25.

17. Jamison, *Sacrificed Wife/Sacrificer's Wife*, p. 163.

18. Jamison, *Sacrificed Wife/Sacrificer's Wife*, p. 169.

19. Giovanna Borradori, cited in N. Vossoughian, 'Conversation with Giovanna Borradori: Derrida, Habermas, and Philosophy in a Time of Terror', interview, 20 January 2004; available at http://www.agglutinations.com/archives/000033.html (accessed 10 February 2005).

20. Derrida, *Acts of Religion*, pp. 360–61.

21. See Aristarkhova, 'Hospitality'.

Ole Bouman *Thank you, Irina. Before we go to the next presentation, may I take the opportunity to ask you a question about your main argument? It's very interesting to see how you shade this whole notion of hospitality according to certain religious, cultural and national differences. You've referred to the French, and the English, and the Germans, and also referred to differences between religions and even between continental mindsets. I think if you continue that argument you could also say that there are even styles of hospitality, there might be fashions of hospitality, and within all these dimensions, we can see many shades exist within this single concept of hospitality. I think that's productive for our debate today, because before we were talking about hospitality as a kind of monolithic thing, and you broke that* *immediately. But there is one thing that might be very interesting also for us, which is how this critique of the European version of hospitality informs the European or Western practice,* vis à vis *culture with a big C. Does it reflect this European version of hospitality which apparently goes no further than tolerance? In Holland, England, Germany, France and maybe even in Mediterranean European states, people talk a lot about the difference between tolerance and indifference, and they are already very proud of defending tolerance and fighting indifference. You take a big step further, saying tolerance is a very poor version of hospitality. It might be a closed kind of world.*

Earlier, I asked the audience to think about dealing with the absence of Nicolas Bourriaud, absent in flesh, but not rhetorically. We have a text here. I did get a proposal, a bold proposal by **Robert Fleck** *to give that lecture, and digest it immediately into something like a critique or a cultural, intellectual context of that speech. Is there anybody who would like to make another proposal? No? Then I'm very happy to invite Robert Fleck to give that speech.*

[However, Robert Fleck wants to read through Bourriaud's speech first]

Maybe, Iara Boubnova, you would like to address the audience with your views on the topic, and your recent experiences.

Manifesta:
Between Host and Guest
Iara Boubnova

I'm in a complicated position here, because what I wanted to do, and what I did in fact, was to put together a collection of notes about different aspects that for me have a connection with the ideas of, firstly, host cities, and, secondly, hospitality. In a way I tend to separate these two things. These notes are about franchising, and they are about domesticity; they are about the advance intelligence that host cities and the system of hospitality usually strive for.

I won't start my talk with distributing thanks either, because I'm in the position of the guest, and guests usually give the thanks at the end. At the beginning they usually have some expectations. So, being a guest, I'm still in the phase of having expectations. However, the moment I come here I change my status, and I turn into something more powerful than a guest. I say all of that because you can see how fragile is the host–guest opposition. It is shifting all the time, and it is changing all the time more specifically whenever contemporary art is concerned. If I am a guest here, nonetheless I would say that I have pretty good experience of being a host. I'm from Sofia, Bulgaria. It's a small country with a very small artistic community. So, for me and the circle of friends and colleagues of mine, we have the pleasure and honour, as well as the obligation, to welcome (on a practically weekly basis) whoever happens to be coming to Sofia with an interest in contemporary art. We are then activating our pretty aggressive hospitality towards those guests, presenting the very specific situation of the country, and presenting ourselves in a system that we would imagine is based on the expectations of our guests.

For me the expectations of the guests and the expectations of the hosts concerning the future of their relationship differ a lot from what we have at hand when discussing Manifesta. Because hospitality is based mainly on conventions and tradition, while Manifesta and Manifesta-triggered relationships are based rather on contracts. Thus what I tried to address in my notes is the question about what is the interaction of the host–guest relationship based on contracts on one side, and hospitality that is based on tradition, on the other.

So, the host–guest duality is probably rooted in the symbolic exchange mechanisms, and it relates back to social relations of old times. As already mentioned, it's changing right now, and it's changing pretty quickly. Ole Bouman feels that The Netherlands is no longer hospitable. I am a representative of a potential emigrant community, and I would say that Holland remains pretty hospitable compared to many other countries. Maybe this is changing much faster than I can follow the situation, but once again the problem of hospitality is the problem of expectations. So, what happens with hospitality in modern times? One has only to think of the automatic urge to bring a gift when paying a visit, or of the 'gift' of extending hospitality when expecting guests. It's impossible to consider the host and the guest separately from each other. A host is only a host when there are guests coming, and vice versa. Hosts and guests are two sides in a social relation and their positions alternate easily; the relation is marked by distinct dynamics. The host–guest opposition is often provisional, yet one is constantly aware of the strengths and weaknesses of each of the two sides. In sport, for instance, there is always reference to the host–guest situation in a game, and we know that in soccer it's very important, when you're winning, whether you're winning as a host or as a guest: you benefit more when you're winning as a guest. The question though is how does that work with contemporary art shows, for example?

In traditional societies there were rules governing the economy of the host–guest exchange. There were accepted procedures and routines of what to do and not to do. Respect could be gained both from being a host and from being an invited guest. The host–guest rules varied in different communities, and these rules had to be negotiated further when there was a cross-community host–guest exchange. The example based on Kant that Irina Aristarkhova gave is very interesting in terms of Manifesta. I would say that Manifesta is trying to approach the relationship to the host locations, or being a host in sports, by way of starting in English, by claiming respect for itself, going on to the French, by being very polite and kind, and finishing generally in German: to quote the quotation from

Irina's presentation: 'The Germans are more hospitable to strangers than any other nation'.

I would say that when we are talking about contemporary art projects and big exhibitions, Manifesta in particular, it seems more adequate to speak about ambassadors rather than guests. In the old times ambassadors were not only political and official representatives, they were a kind of a hostage in the cultures and locations to which they were sent and where they stayed. With their very presence in this specific place, they guaranteed the friendly behaviour of the host and of their own country as well. An ambassador was a special kind of prominent, permanent guest, who could become a host only as a representative of a foreign power on his premises. Embassies are this specific kind of location in other countries, cities, cultures, and traditions. The host–guest duality is always meant to strengthen links in a community of people; plus, you need somebody to negotiate communication between different cultures. Unlike other biennials and this type of art event, Manifesta has different dynamics of the host–guest dualism. In the case of the Istanbul Biennial or Documenta, for instance, the organising committee, usually international in composition and acting on behalf of the host city, invites an outside curator who is at first a guest. By the time of the opening the guest curator is almost a host, but not quite. He or she could be seen as an ambassador figure: invited, in other words – sent by the international art world – and held 'hostage' as a guarantee that the event will have all the relevant markings of an international event of quality and relevance to contemporary art.

On the other side, the guest curator also functions as a guarantee that the host city will extend the necessary level of hospitality to accommodate such an art event. It's also true that most organising committees are composed of both local art personalities and invited international figures. So all of them are hosts and guests, and they are supposed somehow to find a common language. Yet in such events the always identical, though internally changing, host city is a stable constant. With time, the novelty value of such host cities becomes less pronounced, as is the case with Istanbul, for example. In this case the identity of the host is the dominant factor preceding the identity of the guest: you know where you're going, you know how to get there, and you know a little bit of what to expect, at least as a context. The host factor in such cases is more active in defining the relationship, at least in the larger framework, than the characteristics of the guest. In a way, in such events, the host invites a guest about whom it knows nothing beforehand, and on whom it will impose its own identity in the process of exchange. Here the level of advance intelligence concerns only the identity of the invited curator, or artistic director, and his or her professional track record, but not the identity of the resulting art event. On the subject of identities, the Russian artist Yuri Leiderman made a very nice remark few years ago. He said that he felt that when he is invited to participate in exhibitions, especially group shows, it's no longer him in control: it's the curator's expectation of a specific identity that he or she invites. Even if the artist is coming to this show without any particular project and the room is empty, his identity is always already waiting for him there.

I would say that this is very close to what happens with Manifesta. Even though there is no knowledge about the host place, and about the personalities who are to be involved, it's an identity, and the Manifesta identity is the first thing that appears in this host location, which is expecting it. The host city is usually negotiated first. The potential host city must at first recognise itself as a Manifesta host. And then there is this complication of the relationship with Manifesta, because what kind of a host is the one who is expected to invest in being a host, but who willingly discards his right to determine how things will be? All of that means that the host does not have much influence on the curatorial choice; that you can't guarantee that there will be local artists in the show; that you can't intervene in the process of preparation; that you are not doing this and that, etc. Imagine yourself in this situation of hospitality. That's very difficult. That's really a very tough type of hospitality attitude to build up and sustain.

So, Manifesta says: my identity appears first. The label of this dedication to absolute freedom, to novelty, to youth, to dynamics, to investigation of unusual things and situations, this is the thing that is expected to happen on the host side. And if the advance intelligence on the side of the potential host city is already finalised, the host city knows that it can expect the unknown. The well-done homework by the host city, in general, can only confirm the label, the Manifesta trademark, and that's what appears there first.

In other words, a host city for Manifesta is not just any city, but a city that has already perceived itself as having some relevant characteristics, whatever these might be, that are adequate to the Manifesta identity/label/trademark. Or, to put it another way, a Manifesta host city is a city that has always already projected the Manifesta identity onto itself. When we are talking about the Istanbul Biennial, or Documenta, or whatever, these events that are not so active and mobile, we can say: it's the same city but a different event, depending on different curators, topics, political situation and so on. Manifesta 1, 2, 3 and 4, and now Manifesta 5, might all be quite different in character and artistic orientation but from the point of view of the potential host city it is the overall Manifesta label, identity and even aura that matters. It seems that from this point of view the formula for Manifesta is: different cities, same event; but the nature of this sameness is not that easy to define, except that it is, again, travelling, young, active, more open than others (actually nobody knows how *much* more it's open), less marketable than others (nobody is actually commenting on how much *less* marketable it is), and so on.

Once again even the identity of the 'same' event is very specific in the case of Manifesta. Manifesta, by definition, actually constructs its hosts. There is a set of requirements that a potential host city should meet. This is a clear case of the guest constructing the host, although that is a very general statement and it only applies in the initial stages of work on each new Manifesta event. On this general level we can say that the basic identity of the host city is also always already there – as a generalised image, waiting in Amsterdam to be embodied in the flesh and blood of a concrete location. By definition, Manifesta 'knows' its hosts, while the hosts – once they become such by contract – 'know' their guest. However, both 'know' each other on the basis of mutual advance intelligence, on aura(s), and so on. Thus as far as establishing the real and actual host–guest working relationship, well, this is a kind of blind date, at least at the beginning, with all the risks accepted. At this stage the Manifesta host–guest situation is quite complex because neither of the two sides can be entirely sure of its status, as either a host or a guest. They share each other's characteristics and they are connected with each other much more strongly than host and guest normally are. While the city of Istanbul and its biennial, for instance, impose themselves on the guest curator and artists, Manifesta imposes itself on its host city even before either the curator or the artists are selected. The irony is that the only thing the host city knows about the Manifesta event that it wants is that (a) it has decided to host it; and (b) it will be a Manifesta event and nothing else. At this initial stage all the host city knows or cares about is that this is for sure *the* Manifesta; while at the same time feeling quite secure that it actually knows what the Manifesta label or identity is. Thus, we may say that in every potential Manifesta host city there is the Manifesta identity, image and label already waiting to be embodied, consumed and acted out.

Manifesta, though, is unique in view of its specific dual, even triple, procedure of selection. There is the selection of the host city, then the selection of the curatorial team, while the third part of the selection concerns the artists. The position of the Manifesta curator is quite specific too. In the Istanbul Biennial, for instance, the identity, the label and the trademark of the art event coincide with the identity of the city and the curator. In the case of Manifesta there is a split of identities, because the identity of the event is different from the identity of the host city, and actually from the identity of the curators. So, the number one task of the selected curatorial team would be to negotiate or synchronise these two initially separated identities. The Manifesta curator has to negotiate the expectations of both the Manifesta Foundation, in terms of the identity, the brand name, the label and the tradition, and the host city that has identified itself with this label. Plus, there are the artists, for whom the curators eventually become hosts. This is a process of navigation within a very complex environment. Furthermore, I would say that artists are not very typical guests, because normally, what you expect when you invite artists to participate in an event is that they will be ironical, and they will manipulate the context of the situation. Sometimes they are rather more energetic, I would say, towards the context, so one can say that artists are indeed representative of the kind of guest who has been nominated to really get ever more involved.

Once the host city and the curatorial team are selected and contracted, Manifesta is franchised. Among the other meanings of the term, the Merriam-Webster's dictionary defines a franchise as a specific privilege granted to an individual or group, especially the right to be and exercise the powers of a corporation; the right or licence granted to an individual or group to market a company's goods or services in a particular territory; and the territory involved in such a right. The curators are the physical and professional subjects of this franchised enterprise. They are entrusted with hospitality management, although in theory they are guests of both Manifesta and the host city. The curators must put into practice the artistic aspects of the contract between the Manifesta Foundation and the city. This means that they have to translate into art, artists and works, into art event terms, the exchange of characteristics that has already taken place in the contract between the provisional guest, Manifesta, and the provisional host, the host city.

There is however the problem of translation between two opposites: the curators must see Manifesta in this particular city, as well as seeing this particular city in Manifesta. The first part of the task is relatively obvious because all it means is that the curators are exercising their professional capacity in a new location. Presumably their professional capacity has been developed over the years in the context of the international art world. So, this is a kind of domestication of the global. The second part is maybe harder, because it is a kind of globalising of the domestic. And here the experience of having worked in a specific local art scene for a period of time may come in quite handy. Of course, both these words, 'local' and 'global', have some negative connotations. Contemporary art seems to be an urban and a cosmopolitan thing. However, while we seem to know what is urban about contemporary art, it's not so clear what makes contemporary art cosmopolitan. It would appear that the format of Manifesta, its identity, image, way of functioning, is uniquely positioned to elaborate on such issues because the problem is actually the space between different urban centres and art scenes. Actually, the hospitality management referred to here is precisely the activity which negotiates the spaces between different cities and art scenes from the perspective of one single city, the host city. There is no more hospitality as such, there is only the management of hospitality, and it is related to what in a completely different context, not an entirely innocent one, is called 'outsourcing'. Once again, the Merriam-Webster dictionary (I am using it a lot!) defines outsourcing as 'the practice of subcontracting manufacturing work to outside, and especially foreign or non-union companies'. That would be the participating artists. The Manifesta identity and the host city identity that are mediated by the curators and their concepts come together in the figure of the artist, although this is not necessarily reflected in the works, nor in any visible way. It is mainly the potential to recognise the relationship, the management of hospitality, if it has indeed happened.

I think that the basic rule of hospitality management for a Manifesta curator, in collaboration with the artists, is to challenge the hosts, the city as well as the

Manifesta Foundation: to challenge the label and the identity so that neither one is the same after the consummation of the established relations. I remember that when I worked with my colleagues Stéphanie Moisdon Trembley, Nuria Enguita Mayo and Martin Fritz on Manifesta 4 in Frankfurt, one of the host-city-related jokes was nicknaming our project 'Money-festa' – it comes from money, of course. Manifesta 5 is in San Sebastian so I would suggest the nickname 'Mani-fiesta'. That for me is how the situation develops. Thank you!

Ole Bouman *If you allow me, I'll ask you one question, to relate your presentation to the previous one. You are giving a perfect dissection of the ideal body of Manifesta, because the true body of Manifesta sometimes may show some bruises... things can happen in a process that don't completely correspond to this ideal description, but I think it's a perfect attempt to describe the mission behind Manifesta. We all know that this is a European endeavour, it is a European biennale. And in Irina's talk, this Europeanness was analysed in terms of the notion of hospitality and what the Europeans made of it, of the hospitable. So do you think that your description of the role of host cities relates to this Europeanness that is at the core of Irina's argument?*

Iara Boubnova I would say that the word 'tolerance' is much more adequate in the context of this discussion in general. It's not hospitality, it's political tolerance. Here is where one of the first problems appears. I would say that it is not only a problem for Manifesta curators, for I do not speak of everybody's opinion and position. Wherever and whenever you are working outside of your local small community, your friendly situation ... the first thing that appears is the question of tolerance. So maybe hospitality is something which we don't need to discuss too much.

I have even collected some examples which show that the international art event is not as hospitable as it tries to be. For example, distances: how to reach from here to there. I would say that in the case of Frankfurt – the curators never selected this city – Frankfurt is in the upper level of hospitality. From wherever you come to Frankfurt, by flight it's usually direct and fairly cheap. Whenever it's a more exotic place, even if it's interesting, it tends to be much more expensive. Then it's less hospitable, in these terms.

Ole Bouman *We have another presentation, as you know, it is Robert Fleck's intervention.*

Robert Fleck I must say, it was quite a misunderstanding because I thought, of course, that this text would be in French, so I thought it would be easiest not to read it in French, but to give a kind of abstract talk. And now I discover that this text is in English, and so I just want to read it. It's not very long, but first perhaps to say one thing, that the topic of hospitality is also very close to the absence of **Nicolas Bourriaud** today, because he is at the Palais de Tokyo, which he founded with

Jerome Sans in 2000. He is a host in one of the buildings of the French State, but they will have to leave their position in the building in January 2005. So even the visit today by the owner of the building, the French minister of culture, to his institution, is also ambiguous. And just to say that, of course, they are hosts in their own institution, and now they are being thrown out. And perhaps we once had a kind of utopian idea that it would be very nice to host the Palais de Tokyo in different institutions in Europe after they were thrown out in Paris next January. So, here is the text of Nicolas in English. I will just read it.

Nicolas Bourriaud

First, I would like to apologise for not having been able to come. An unexpected event obliges me to stay in Paris today. Nevertheless, I really wanted to write those few words as a contribution to your debate, and I hope its reader will be kind enough to correct my bad English.

Hosting is a curator's problem – a major one, especially if, as I am at the Palais de Tokyo, you are heading an institution which has to care about people having lunch or dinner, buying books or editions besides the exhibitions. But I think the main interest I take in this theme concerns the artist. In my book *Relational Aesthetics* I attempt to focus on and articulate a problematic that has been outlined since the beginning of the nineties by such artists as Rirkrit Tiravanija, Douglas Gordon, Pierre Huyghe, Gabriel Orozco, Angela Bulloch, Vanessa Beecroft, Philippe Parreno and Christine Hill, among many others – and, of course, Felix Gonzalez-Torres, whose work perfectly embodies what I want to call 'relational aesthetics'.

Let us recall the basic, simplified definitions. What I named *relational art* is a set of artistic practices that use the interpersonal sphere as their theoretical and practical starting point. Relational aesthetics is also an aesthetic theory that evaluates a work of art according to the interpersonal relations that it depicts, produces or models. This theory has roots that are simultaneously sociological, political, aesthetic, psychological and philosophical. *Sociological*: because our era can be characterised by the restructuring of its industries according to the new tools of communication and service (the Internet). The artists subscribing to this aesthetic struggle against the institutional interactivity that the Gatesian dream of an 'information highway' typifies and against the impoverishing homogenisation of the forms of social interaction we are offered. Hence *political*: after sweeping away the avant-garde, radical politics was reformulated from notions of proximity and micro-utopia (recreate the world according to relations of vicinity, and no longer from abstract ideas of society). And, of course, *aesthetic*: the consideration, over the course of the nineties, of Fluxus's plastic vocabulary or of performance in the sixties and seventies became a set of formal tools that could be reactivated and recharged with new elements. *Psychological*: as Cooper said, 'Madness is not "in" a person, but in the system of relations in which he or she participates.' And finally *philosophical*: these origins are found in the work of Karl Marx, who explained that the essence of humanity is nothing more than the ensemble of human relations. I was also very much influenced by a little known text by Louis Althusser, one of his last, called 'The Materialism of the Encounter'. It envisions the world as arbitrary and chaotic; and since there is no ontological finality, this lets us transform it.

How does contemporary art reflect the shape of our 'being-together'? Can we still communicate with each other? Those are the crucial questions addressed in the book. And I would add this one: can we envisage a type of globalisation other than that based on the circuits of the market?

I take as an example the work of Rirkrit Tiravanija: each of his artworks is called *Untitled*, adding the different elements of which it is composed, and, last but not least, the words *lots of people*. His works include us within a structure. He literally is the host, welcoming the visitors not as colourspots in a composition, but as active components of the work. 'Hosting' in this sense means sharing time and space with other people – just as when you invite friends for dinner: they are not supposed to come to admire the objects you have acquired or made, but to share an experience. (Except, maybe, at some creepy collectors' dinner parties.) Most of the major artworks of recent years ask us to experience something, rather than *acquiring* a visual stimulus. In 1998, when Carsten Höller proposed as an artwork the absorption of his 'love drug' (a synthetic recomposition of the enzymes that hit our brains when we are in love), he was hosting us in the home of experience.

And I think that *experiencing* the artwork implies something important, which is real time: as a visitor to the exhibition, I am sharing a space-time with the artist. To make myself understood, I can take the example of Philippe Parreno's work. The playground soccer player, one of the many recurrent 'conceptual characters' in his work, was inspired by a true story from the artist's background. As a child, he and his friends would kick the ball while simultaneously delivering a commentary on their own performance, as if in a sports broadcast. Situational model: action and commentary in real time. What space is produced when they are out of sync? How does the form relate to its own deferred (and thus differentiated) self? It is this *deferment* (and thus differential) in regard to reality that determines the *labour power* of the image, which is the main subject of Parreno's work.

Let us go back to Tiravanija, and let us remind ourselves that he is a Buddhist. In Thailand, monks have to be given food by the people; they don't work, at least not in the way we envision working. The gift is undermined in the act of hosting. Felix Gonzalez-Torres embodied this idea of art with his *stacks* that the visitor could take away.

If our generation seems to be depoliticised, it is perhaps because we are waiting
for forms of organisation. The Greek *agora*, the soviets, sit-ins or the assembly
are all relational and political formations. The French Revolution or the soviets
produced formations that were then used in the democratic process. An
association such as Act Up today can take political action because it has invented
its own forms of intervention (the 'zap', for example). We are all waiting for new
collective constructions, not for new utopias.

But if we line up the most innovative works of the last ten years, we can see that
they draw up a plan for another society, piece by piece, sector by sector. The
importance of domesticity in the recent history of art also comes from the fact
that the home has become the main site of experience. And the artwork itself has
become a set, a platform for activities.

Reprogramming existing works, inhabiting historicised styles and forms in the
same way that a lodger inhabits his or her house, is a metaphor for making use of
images and, more generally, exploiting society as a repository of templates.
Together these constitute one of the answers returned by today's artists to a
commodification regime that focuses solely on notions of originality and novelty.

Ole Bouman *I think it's even better to have this presented by a third party, because
its focus on the relational is an attempt to overcome the dialectics between the host
and the guest, as we have been discussing. Maybe that's a good starting point for a
discussion. Have you any questions or comments or additional remarks to make on
the subject?*

Maria Hlavajova I have a question to the three panellists, maybe Robert is willing to
join in. How does the invitation possibly change the concept of hospitality? In other
words, does the act of inviting change our behaviour, our act of being hospitable?
Do we behave differently to guests whom we invite, than to those who invite
themselves? So that would be my question, is the concept of invitation changing the
way we should talk of hospitality or not?

Ole Bouman *Well, it occurs to me as a conceptual question, which might be a perfect
match for Irina to respond to.*

Irina Aristarkhova I think I understand the question you are asking: whether as a
guest, one acts differently or behaves differently if one is invited, versus when one is
not invited. Specifically I think it is different in different contexts. If you are talking
about the text which I referred to, the Sanskrit edition, I think the invitation is a way
out – it's been written before – a way to somehow mediate this relationship between
the host and the guest. It produces a certain distance or hope that the guest will
already be cordoned off – like when you have an invitation stating come at six o'clock
instead of just simply come. In the Sanskrit texts I referred to, I think that that

concept would be considered unnecessary because there are strict rules on what kind of guest can come, what time, according to your age, your social position, your cultural position. On the other hand, within European cultures there are huge differences between the ways in which we treat an invitation. I would like to just give you a couple of anecdotes.

I have a Puerto Rican friend who says that her house can be full of people who come over and just stay. You know, you invite them and they stay around the whole day, and you have to entertain them. And she said that when she first moved to the US, she was shocked to see on an invitation that she was being invited to such and such an event, and the event is between 4 and 6. She said that it came as a shock to her that an invitation itself can provide a framework by which you set a time when the guest basically has to leave, or has to be kicked out. So for her it was a cultural shock in that sense. And again the issue here is whether as host, your behaviour changes if you have guests around, or not. I understand that the European problem, or the Western problem, is that we don't want to change our behaviour. We say, yes you come here as long as I don't have to change my lifestyle. We have it in Moscow, for example. We are fine, we are very hospitable, as long as we don't see you – Chechens or any other ones who don't look like me – around on our streets. We don't want to change our behaviour, and I think that that's definitely a very interesting point.

Ole Bouman *Maybe, just for my information – why did you ask that question? Is there a secret agenda? Do you have any experiences?*

Maria Hlavajova I don't know whether there's a secret agenda. It has to do with a project that I'm preparing called 'Cordially Invited', and it has to do with recent happenings in the Netherlands when 26,000 asylum seekers are being expelled from the country, and 25,000 East European guest workers are invited to come over. That's the cordial invitation, so you are invited, but only under certain conditions. So you have a shower and you put good clothes on, and you deliver work that our people can't provide. The project was within the framework of the Dutch presidency of the European Union, that critically discusses what is New Europe, so to speak. That's why I looked at the notion of hospitality, and I do think that Derrida's notion of unconditional hospitality, when you say yes, no matter what the conditions, is not practically applicable. I could not imagine it. We just came to the conclusion that it's a beautifully abstract notion of hospitality. But I was searching for an interesting way to regulate hospitality as such, and indeed an invitation has this regulatory function. But then the negative aspect comes in, of conditioning your hospitality. And I do think it's about hospitality and not tolerance, by the way.

Ole Bouman *It's an interesting distinction between universal hospitality, the universal invitation, for instance, which resides in the Geneva Convention. It's a universal invitation, you can come if you need us, and there are very strict and specified invitations which have a time regime behind it. I think that might also be worked out later. Is there any other…*

Enrico Lunghi Yes, I would just like to continue with this idea... because I think for me, one of the important differences between tolerance and hospitality is that hospitality includes the willingness to change, as part of a process. In an ideal way, I imagine that when you host something, the guest–host relation is a transforming process, and it's not that afterwards everybody goes home again and nothing has changed. Ideally something should happen, and everybody, the host and the guest, should be at least a little bit different and leave something different for the other. I take the example of Manifesta 2 in Luxembourg. Actually Luxembourg hosted Manifesta – with all the contradictions that Iara pointed out, as to who is the host and who is the guest, and so on – but I think Manifesta changed the situation. Whatever was willing to change, was in the process of changing, but Manifesta helped this change as well. Maybe idealistically, I hope that Manifesta 2 also changed Manifesta a little bit.

Ole Bouman *Did it change Luxembourg for better or for worse?*

Enrico Lunghi Both, somehow. I mean, what does it mean, better or worse? We should then describe a lot of things – how it was before and how it is now. I would say that, talking now only about the Casino [Luxembourg], it allowed us to change our way of working, our possibilities. The Casino was only two years old when it hosted Manifesta, and we were still struggling for our survival. After four years it was settled, and we often referred to Manifesta as an important project that helped to establish the Casino. So in this case, we can say it was very good. In another way I could also say that a lot of people from the outside, when they think about Luxembourg, only think about Manifesta, and they forget that the Casino and the gallery situation in Luxembourg has changed a lot since then, that this is an ongoing process.

Ole Bouman *I like the idea that 1 + 1 is 3. That the whole is more than the sum of its parts. This interpretation is very important to see how hospitality – but also how being a guest – actually helps changing situations, but then we have to discuss what the change is about. You said also you were wondering whether Luxembourg was changing Manifesta at large. Is it true, Henry Meyric Hughes, that Manifesta as an idea is changing over the years with major steps every two years when there is a new instalment?*

Henry Meyric Hughes It's very hard to say. I was going to go back one step, and I will say that because I think the idea of hospitality, of exchange, is that it is not a purely selfish exchange, such as Derrida defines it. I mean, there is the other notion of hospitality, which is the generation of excess value, of super-abundance. It's the unpredictable element, and it's the creation of a larger field of energy than the two which have come together, and I think in those terms both that it has changed Manifesta and that Manifesta has changed in its different manifestations. Because what happens is there is always the element of unpredictability, and this is built into the whole operation of Manifesta. It is about venturing into the fields of unpredictability. We predetermine a certain kind of framework, and beyond that we also predetermine what we can't tell will happen. I don't know if that says anything significant, but there's no question at all that it has changed our attitude. The fact that we're all here today, the fact that we have ancillary programmes, that we've realised that it's an idea which doesn't start and stop but actually grows and expands and changes shape is very important.

Ole Bouman *I guess this very event, a Coffee Break, is a new phenomenon within the larger framework.*

Rob MacDonald My name is Rob MacDonald, I'm an architect from Liverpool. I'm very interested in this concept of the unexplained guest, the uninvited guest. We've spoken about the kind of host and the guest, but hosts and guests are almost bio-medical terms that refer to the host's body and the guest invading the host's body. So, I think that there's another term, a parasite, which is quite an interesting concept, and I think that there is a role for the parasite in the artistic process of creation. One of the groups that I did have some contact with a year or so ago were Fluxus, and I think Fluxus create amazing events and – a 1960s' word – 'happenings' that are very positive and very creative. I'm really interested in this notion of the uninvited guest, the accidental guest, the ghost that emerges, or Bertolt Brecht's off-stage character that steps onto the stage, and nobody is expecting them, and I think that's really what host and guest is about. It's about creating a space for creativity and for the uninvited, unexplained kind of guest.

Ole Bouman *A surprise, a space for surprises. Anyone else? Robert?*

Robert Fleck I would say this would just explain this very important distinction between invitation and hospitality. In fact we were thinking, after the text of Nicolas Bourriaud, why he didn't speak about his own curatorial practice. And in fact, in the text, which I had the opportunity to read twice, it's very interesting that he didn't talk about his own curatorial practice as hospitality. So in fact he didn't mix it up because when he talked about hospitality as his curatorial task in an institution, he was talking about the visitor and about people having dinner in his museum and so on. And he was not making this confusion, and I think it's very important that the normal way to behave in a museum is to invite an artist, the artist is not the unexpected guest. And to invite is always to make a selection and to exclude, in fact, all the other people. If you decide about a monographic exhibition then it's a very hard decision because you exclude all the other artists. Even, for instance, if you decide to make an exhibition with Mike Kelley, you decide immediately not to make an exhibition with Paul McCarthy. So it's really hard not to say, oh, we are very hospitable, just because we are inviting artists. But at the same time, in the text of Nicolas, it's also interesting that he is referring mainly to two artists in his idea of hospitality, Rirkrit Tiravanija and Felix Gonzalez-Torres, who are non-European and non-American artists in the way that they come from other cultures, and in fact they have another practice. They really introduce the unexpected guest; who was, I think, not really inside of Fluxus, because Fluxus is a small community. This idea to use the public to create the unexpected guest is very strong for Tiravanija and Gonzalez-Torres.

Ole Bouman *So, hospitality as an act of inclusion. But if there is a negative, another side of that it's also an act of exclusion. Do you think we should be aware of that, inviting artists but also inviting people for projects? Do you think this conscience about both sides of the question is highly important?*

Robert Fleck In a way, not to say we are extremely altruistic, just because we are inviting artists. For instance, in Germany there's a word very much used in the museum world, it's an incredible word, it's *Besucherfreundlichkeit*, and if you compare it to hospitality in a very strict sense, as you explained it, it's pure ideology, it's like saying 'friendliness to the visitor'. If you say this is hospitality, then we are in complete confusion and only producing ideology, and it's very important to avoid this, I think.

Ole Bouman *A funny thing, that in the computer industry you have this notion of user-friendly, and the most user-friendly devices are the ones with closed codes; an open source is most of the time very unfriendly to use if you want to get into open source software... they're getting better, but it's going very slowly...*

Jean Grant My name is Jean Grant, I'm a local artist. It seems that in one part of our discussion we are talking about the need for humans to see each other as equal, and yet it also seems that hospitality is about the dehumanisation of one of the partners, and that tolerance is also about the dehumanisation of one of the partners. I wonder if it's possible for humans who regard themselves as equal to be hospitable?

Irina Aristarkhova I don't think of it in terms of going out and looking at other cultures and immigrants as refugees. I think that we have a lot of work to do at home as well, in that sense.

Robert Fleck I suspect that the word we're not using, but we're kind of stalking, is the word 'power'. And perhaps one of the things we really do know is that we've not yet been brought up from an early age to develop sufficiently a sense of self-critical reflexivity around power and all its manifestations in us. Not just the power differentials of access, not just the power differences, but the deep-seated stuff which I think Irina was alluding to in her presentation, around ethnicity, around gender, etc. And I think a lot of that is what is left implicit, in terms of who issues invitations, and about our ability to offer hospitality. Perhaps we can't offer the hospitality unless we make a bigger effort to know who we are and how we've got to be where we are at any particular historical and cultural point in time. So, I find myself constantly, wherever I go, not begging, not pleading, but hoping that people will actually start to do that work, which is not only about the other, but it's about ourselves. And those with power, of course, don't want to do that work. So we have to examine what our own power is, and see how we're positioned within those power relations, whether it's an institution or a nation state. And therefore what our responsibility is, and how we can imaginatively and humanely work with it.

Ole Bouman *It sounds very sympathetic, and I think most people will agree with you that this kind of self-reflection is highly important... but on the other hand, if you* *think about the different interventions, for instance, maybe all of them, they do reflect that kind of reflexivity. There is this notion of power, heavily represented in different discourses, don't you think? So if we think about hospitality as an act of exclusion, or hospitality as something which has a time limit, or hospitality as another word for tolerance, which is a kind of negative freedom and nothing else, there is already an incredible amount of reflexivity.*

Robert Fleck It can be kept very much at the abstract level. It's about how it changes, how we enact our relations with each other, whether it's professionally or personally. That's the difficult bit. Pulling our weight.

Ole Bouman *One more thing. Could it be possible that self-criticism and reflexivity might also be a hindrance to hospitality, because it's about the self again?*

Robert Fleck Critical self-reflexivity is not a self-indulgence, and I didn't use the word 'criticism'. Critical self-reflexivity. It's not an indulgence, and it's not just about the self. It is about the self in all its many contexts. It's not a private but a political process.

Member of the audience I'm glad about the demand for hard work because I agree that working with notions like hospitality or tolerance for others, especially if they're linked to very imminent but complex political questions, of course, if one takes it seriously it always ends with hard work, which takes years. I would like to propose a notion that helps maybe doing that work in very practical fields, like exhibition-making, because what is happening here, in whatever use of the word – the European, or, as Irina spelt it out, in the Asian one, which I'm not so familiar with – I think it's always about a set of rules. So the notion, however you use it, is never just a notion that answers all the affiliated questions. So it's not about hospitality and then everybody knows, oh, that's hospitality. It defines, and this is also history, at least in Europe, its legal sense. It has the sense of a very specific set of rules, regulations, rights, orders, all kinds of things that are attached to the notion. So, if we look at this part of the history, and that's the story about the invitation which specifies from 4 to 6, it's a small story of civilisations... In the absence of gods, or in the absence of deities, or in the absence of other codifications which come out of local customs, or power relations, of course those regulations and rules need to be set anew, negotiated anew, and filled with life. So, that set of rules needs to be worked on very practically. That's what I also think needs to be done, if I think about the relation of artists and institutions: it's not about just a catch-all notion, where either side takes the benefit of each role. So the institution would say, I'm a host and that's a great position. And the artist would say, yes but I'm a guest and that's also a great position. And the host can only say, I open my door; you can do whatever you want. And the guest says, oh great, I'm a guest; I can do whatever I want. That was never, ever the case in notions like hospitality. It's about a complex set of rules. We alone could spend two weeks just finding out which set of rules could apply, for example, to the artist/institutional relationship of Manifesta. So my question would be: which set of rules would anybody here propose for his or her work? Because if we just think we can solve it by one notion, and look at it as some kind of open door for complete liberty, which we all know does not exist, then we'll be on the wrong track. There is a German saying from medieval times: that the guest, like fish, starts to stink after three days.

Ole Bouman *Yes, I think it's good to jump to the practical level, although I have a feeling there is a kind of shared desire that people would like to dig into the substance underneath the rules, which is about mentality and attitude...*

Henry Meyric Hughes Just one or two more comments. Before we leave the 4 to 6 thing, there's a nice expression in English which is, of course, that a guest might outstay his or her welcome. Being a guest has reciprocal obligations, obviously, and that's what we're talking about in part. What I would like to go back to is your comment about Nicolas Bourriaud's programme at the Palais de Tokyo, when he talks about the food actually. In a certain sense this is part of the new aesthetic, and what his approach and the approach of many artists in the nineties brings, I think, is a much heightened awareness of not just the host and the guest in the sense of institution and artist, but audience and its involvement of ordinary people, and the obligation in the way that they are invited to complete a work of art in the Duchampian sense, which I think is part of the discussion we're having today.

■ ■ ■ ■ ■ ■ ■ ■ ■

Jeanne van Heeswijk Just a small remark, because we talk a lot about the host and about power, and you talk about a set of rules. I think if we talk about hospitality we should also take into account that it is also a mutual set of expectations, which is different than only rules. It's that both the host and the guest expect something from each other, and I think it's in matching or trying to match this expectation where there is a lot of possibility for negotiation and also possibility for change, more than in a set of rules. So, I think more important than a set of rules is a set of expectations you bring to the table. And even the notion of the unexpected guest – sometimes you can also say the unexpected guest itself has a certain expectation from the host by being unexpected. I think that's very important, to take into account that the guest in that sense is not innocent, and the host is also not only giving in that sense.

Ole Bouman *I think that's a good point. But we also discussed in Amsterdam, some months ago, that there is also a heavy psychological dimension in this. Where there are guests and hosts there are expectations, and when there are expectations there are frustrations, and unmatched expectations, which is most of the time the substance of lots of gossip and also complaints.*

Member of the audience What I'm missing in this discussion is the concept of vulnerability. When you invite somebody into your house you are also in a weak position, and only now am I becoming aware of the importance of Irina's speech, where she really makes things very drastic, talking about eating sons and things like that. But I think especially for Manifesta, it's an interesting situation, because here you're dealing with inviting artists. And artists are not your usual guests, I guess, because what you're actually wanting from them is something else, you're not sitting having tea cosily, and stuff like that, you're actually inviting people who unsettle things, and who are maybe bringing something that might pose a danger to the situation. And because everybody's talking about power – maybe it's a personal thing, but for me art and hospitality have always been mutually exclusive, because my parents had a very large art collection, and I never had any friends over because they might destroy something. So I want to introduce the notion of the danger... there's a real danger when you bring in Manifesta. There's another level where the curators become really radical and invite artists who start pissing against the mayor's house, and the mayor's not so happy about that, but he invited them, so what's he going to do about this, and I think that's interesting to Manifesta, being a traveller itself.

Ole Bouman *That might be a side-effect of relational aesthetics, that you don't have that problem of damage and not inviting people any longer because you are afraid of damage.*

Member of the audience That's the interesting thing. They are inviting, but at the same time they know there might be a danger. And especially in San Sebastian I think that's a very interesting political arena, and this might be even more important.

Anders Harm Hello. I'm from Tallinn, and I wanted to add to the previous statement. I wanted to say from my position or my experience, I would say that there is no uninvited guest, in the case of a municipality asking for a contemporary art project. It's pre-programmed that something might happen. The municipality is symbolically over this, with little symbolical quarrels between one artist and the whole project. It's hosting the whole thing, it takes into account the possibility of the radicality of someone, and that's what makes it important. First applying the role of a host, being taken into hostage, like Iara Boubnova said, and then again getting released, there's a power position, there's a vulnerability position, so I guess it's like ping-pong.

Ole Bouman *Yes, I think it's a good additional remark to the previous one. My question would be to both of you, actually: if this element of the vulnerable or the unconditional, which are related to some extent, are just elements that are forgotten, are you blaming this discourse, but also larger discourses, for forgetting that element? Or are you dreaming and do you have something specific in mind, of changing a certain practice in which these elements could be embodied?*

Of course, to some extent this opens a whole new discussion. On the other hand there is already a lot of debate on art which is not invited, appropriation art, free work, even. Artists get inspired without any invitation and they make work; sometimes this work is outside and it happens, so it does exist. I don't know whether from the other side, from the angle of the host, there is a kind of similar practice that can be defined. I guess so. A kind of free hosting, without knowing who will be the invitees, but I think that might be an interesting... you want to ask something?

Member of the audience It doesn't bring along the notion of guest, I mean in the case of appropriation art – something you have appropriated… is the person who is appropriating actually the guest of an earlier cultural heritage?

Ole Bouman *I do know that much of appropriation art very soon becomes the art of the guest, which was heavily discussed in the sixties and seventies; it was called the technique of repressive tolerance, encapsulating the art, and as soon as it is encapsulated it becomes a guest of something larger, which at the same time is at the cost of its power. Anyway, that's maybe too big a topic…*

Member of the audience I think that the issues that were brought up, vulnerability, expectation, they are all of course very important – power, too. When I hear this I can't help think of Derrida's notion of hospitality, when he says to be a host is to have a door, and someone has the key and it's usually not the guest. But I wonder if Manifesta has a very particular and very unique relationship to hosting and guesting in the sense that unlike biennales and the Documenta, or other large-scale events which are always attached to a particular city, Manifesta is always a guest. A guest of a city which has its own set of expectations, and in being a guest it's also a host which invites artists. And there's another set of expectations between Manifesta and the artists. So, at some moment the Über-host, the city itself, may not be happy with the way that Manifesta has conveyed into being this middle person, this guest that's a host.

Ole Bouman *Manifesta, can you take minutes of this new concept: Über-host. I like this one…*

Robert Fleck I was very sensitive to the questions about vulnerability, and all this, but I think we have not forgotten, I think it has been said somehow during this discussion, we are dealing in the world of art which is not political, which is not social, which is a very specific sphere of human activity. There are people who study the behaviour of cultures, and so anthropologists who are looking at what is the essence itself of hospitality, and how we change due to various conditions, cultural but also as civilisation and also of context. There were studies done, I think in the sixties – for instance in the Nordic countries it was said in the sixties, in the studies I have read, that people were more hospitable than for instance in Paris. But there is really an anthropological reason for this. When your only neighbour is ten kilometres away you are more happy to see him than in Paris where you have neighbours downstairs and all around you. So also these anthropological things are very important. But just to add something to the vulnerability aspect, I think there is also one important moment in the guest–host relation. It is when you leave, when you separate after the hosting. For instance, if you take the Greek stories – I was very surprised when I read this – when a person, a traveller, comes to a king or whoever to stay three months or two years, when he leaves, the host gives him presents, to take away. So I was saying, that's strange, because since he was living as a guest, he should give a present to the host. But it was the opposite. Until it became clear that it is because the one who leaves keeps remembering, and can talk about his host, and say, oh, I was there, and it was wonderful to be there, and it was something very important, an important experience. But this was also possible in a time when people didn't travel a lot. The question also about host and guest today is maybe so complicated because we are all travelling all the time. As it was said before, sometimes we don't know who is really the host and the guest, because maybe I invite an artist or a curator or a lecturer, but the day after, I'm invited back by him, and so where is the limit? And this makes things complicated. So this situation – historical, in terms of civilisation, and anthropological – is very important in this discussion.

Ole Bouman *Sounds like the anthropology of the network society, where the carousel of travelling is going so fast that you see guests that were your hosts only a few hours ago, a few days ago, a couple of weeks ago, and vice versa. An ongoing process which is inevitably blurring the lines... and another form of overcoming these dialectics that we try to stick to, for argument's sake. We need the dialectics because we need an argument.*

I think we are about to come to a full glossary of discussion – not full, about to be full: one more...

Member of the audience I think another point which hasn't been made is about threshold, in the context that it's physical as well as sociological. Yet without threshold there is no guest, there is no host.

Ole Bouman *It's also architecture... Right, well as I said it's a glossary, it's a grey glossary, I guess, probably with lots of white spots, but we can work with this, no doubt about it. I will not try to make a conclusion out of this. So thank you very much again. Time for drinks, wine even. Have a nice evening.*

Occupation: Unknown

Liverpool Biennial and The International Foundation Manifesta are delighted to invite you to the third

Manifesta Coffee Break:
Occupation: Unknown

on 1 and 2 October 2004 to coincide with the third Liverpool Biennial.

This third edition of the Manifesta Coffee Break discusses 'occupation' as a concept that is operational not only within situations of conflict but also outside of them as the object of resistance and a visa requirement. It is the bread and butter of our daily lives and the playing field of freedom fighters. 'Occupation' denotes an originary separation and the desire to possess; it is as much a state of mind as a territorial invasion. In a newly unified Europe, 'occupation' is clouded in hush-hush, recast as a colonial antic or legislated beyond the reach of our new brethren in the accession countries. 'Occupation' is deployed as a development tool, an unfortunate phase towards a certain democracy and human rights. It may also shine a new light upon the privatisation of public spaces. In remembering the temporality of occupation, of what is 'other', we may sense the potential for transformation.

Manifesta Coffee Break takes place on Friday 1 and Saturday 2 October 2004. Chaired by Declan McGonagle, Professor of Art and Design at the University of Ulster and chairman of Liverpool Biennial, the Friday programme will be open to the public. On Saturday, there is the opportunity for more intensive discussion in four workshops around the aspects of occupation discussed by the speakers. These workshops are by invitation only; apart from you, we are inviting artists, curators and other cultural practitioners. The proceedings will be used as the basis for a publication to appear in spring 2005.

Manifesta Coffee Break is organised by Liverpool Biennial in cooperation with International Foundation Manifesta (IFM) as part of the Manifesta New Network Programme 2002–2005 supported by the Culture 2000 programme of the European Union. The Network Programme also includes the Manifesta Biennial, the Manifesta Archives, and the *Manifesta Journal*. (www.manifesta.nl)

On a practical level, we can offer you expenses for economy (air) travel and transfers as well as hotel accommodation for two nights in Liverpool's Adelphi Hotel. There are 30 places available, which will be allocated on a first come, first served basis. To confirm your attendance please return attached booking form to Lorna Woods Moses.

We very much hope you are willing and able to accept our invitation and look forward to hearing from you.

Yours sincerely,

Paul Domela   Hedwig Fijen
Deputy Chief Executive   Director
Liverpool Biennial   International Foundation Manifesta

Coffee Break Steering Group: Paul Domela (Liverpool Biennial), Ole Bouman (editor, *Archis*), Declan McGonagle (University of Ulster), Hedwig Fijen (IFM), Yiannis Toumazis (general coordinator, Manifesta 6, Nicosia)

Occupation: Unknown concludes a three-part series of discussions around visual art and contemporary curatorial practice in a changing Europe. Previous discussions focused on the concepts of refugee and hospitality.

The Privatisation of Public Space[1]
Anna Minton

I. The Privatisation of Public Space

Change is coming to Liverpool but the city is divided about what the future holds. Alongside the news that Liverpool is to be 'Capital of Culture' in 2008 a new £750 million regeneration scheme plans to privatise the city centre, raising fears about the future of public space in the city.

The Paradise Street Development Area, which includes thirty-four streets, is to be entirely privatised, managed by developer Grosvenor Estates, policed by its own security force, and ruled by its own laws. Traditional rights of way are to be replaced by special 'public realm arrangements' which will be policed by 'quartermasters' or 'sheriffs'. Begging, skating and rollerblading will be banned and no demonstrations will be allowed without police permission. The aim is to transform what is a relatively run-down city centre into a complex of luxury apartments, high quality shopping, recreation and leisure facilities.

For the people of Liverpool, the potential resurgence of the city is surely a good thing. However, headlines in newspapers such as *The Sunday Times* accusing Grosvenor Estates of eroding civil liberties reflect more widespread concerns, with organisations ranging from human rights group Liberty to the Open Spaces Society voicing fears about the implications of private management wresting control of public spaces.

The scheme has only just got the go-ahead and with the first foundations still to be laid it will be a few years until the impact of the proposals is properly felt and understood. But what is already clear is that this example is part of more widespread trends towards the privatisation of public space in cities. In Liverpool the private management of the streets reflects the particular leasing arrangements agreed between Grosvenor and the city council. While these arrangements are particular to Liverpool they clearly also share a lot in common with the introduction of Business Improvement Districts (BIDs), an American regeneration policy which has recently received parliamentary approval in the UK.

In the US BIDs have proved very controversial. While their introduction has been seen as integral to the clean-up of New York, they are also deemed responsible for growing polarisation in cities. In New York, for example, the Grand Central BID made the front page of the *New York Times* when an article alleged that the homeless were being beaten up and driven off the private and public areas covered by the BID. In many other US cities too the presence of marginal groups, such as homeless people, on private sector property managed by the BIDs is a point of contention. This clearly echoes Grosvenor's plans to ban certain groups and certain behaviours from their property.

It is too early to predict accurately what the impact of these trends towards privatisation will be in the UK. However, the nature and feel of earlier similar schemes, such as Exchange Square in London's Broadgate development, give some indication of the likely sterility and lack of diversity of these carefully controlled environments. While the UK is unlikely to replicate exactly the American model, the 'Disneyfication' of, for example, Times Square in New York also gives some indication of the effects of corporate dominance over public space.

II. Privatisation, Gating and Crime

As these trends towards the privatisation of public space gather pace a similar movement towards the privatisation of residential development is, if anything, further ahead. This is most clearly manifested in the US, where 15 per cent of the population live in gated communities, while at the other end of the spectrum the same number are trapped in ghettoes of exclusion. Gating – side by side with ghettoes of exclusion – is also particularly prevalent in other societies with very significant disparities between rich and poor, in Latin America, South Africa and South East Asia.

Like the privatisation of public space, the rise of gating also has profound implications for public life and the future of democracy, as people opt out of local government in favour of the privatised services on offer behind their gates. In the US at least five communities have incorporated as independent entities, entirely independent of local government and hence the requirement to pay local taxes. The consequence is that the locally collected tax base shrinks further, ensuring that local government services drop in standard and further encouraging the local population – increasingly referred to as citizen-consumers – to opt for privatised services. Of course, the problem with this is that decent quality private services will only be an option for those who can afford them. Those who cannot will have no choice but to rely on an increasingly struggling public sector, more and more polarised from its private counterpart.

Aside from democratic concerns, the other key impact of the privatisation of both public and residential space is its relationship with crime and in particular perceptions of crime. A growing body of evidence indicates that while areas may be 'forting up', ubiquitous signs of security, such as fences, electronic surveillance and security guards, actually enhance fears of crime rather than providing reassurance. In both the US and Britain crime has actually fallen over the last decade but the perception among 90 per cent of Americans is that it is getting worse, while a resounding 70 per cent in the UK also mistakenly take this view.

It would seem that this perception of rising crime is linked to the wider polarisation, taking place in society as a whole, in which dislocated groups harbour suspicions of each other. A key reason for this is likely to be the discomfort caused by ever more visible signs of polarisation, with areas of deprivation just a stone's throw from gates and guards. London's Canary Wharf, where the growing finance district sits side by side with some of the most deprived estates in the capital, is a prime example.

Such responses are borne out by research from California which has shown that while a group of homeless people in Berkeley were involved in absolutely no criminal behaviour at all, the area they congregated in was mistakenly associated with high levels of crime by their wealthier neighbours, leading to a permanent climate of mutual distrust between the two groups.

Then of course there is also the fact that the growth of private security raises concerns about the future of the police as a public service. In the US, private security outstrips spending on public law enforcement by an astonishing 73 per cent and in Miami 19 per cent of streets are not covered by police. This is clearly not a situation conducive to public safety since Miami is also the murder capital of the US.

III. The Postmodern City

Just as modernism considered the city to be the primary locus of modernity, so today social commentators talk of the postmodern as the metropolitan. But where modernity concerned itself with the fractures caused by industrial production, today postmodernity is concerned with the social changes of late capitalism and the accompanying rise of services and consumerism. So the city is seen as the site of the consumerist, Disneyfied world, as de-industrialisation continues to turn cities into centres of consumption, boosted by iconic buildings, museums and creative quarters.

What is happening in Liverpool and in towns and cities around the UK can be seen in this context, as cities compete with each other, with the backing of private finance, to create the most appealing 'downtowns' in the lofts and warehouses of the former industrial city. These centres of consumption are designed as residential and leisure playgrounds to attract the 'knowledge workers' of the highly paid, globally connected service industries.

As already outlined, there are a number of dangers posed by the creation of such privatised enclaves, not least the sterility of the resulting environment. The exclusion of not merely beggars and rollerbladers but large parts of the population, who live in deprived estates on the peripheries of such cities, is the other major concern as more and more towns and cities exhibit growing signs of these 'two-speed economies'. In a city such as Liverpool, which has high levels of unemployment and deprivation, particularly in outlying districts, this is a particular problem.

Issues such as this are also at the heart of debates perennially surrounding the accolade of 'Capital of Culture'. Whether or not 'Capital of Culture' will genuinely involve the city's population as a whole or whether it will be just another manifestation of economic boosterism, with no benefits to or participation by the outlying community – or even the non-mainstream artistic community – remains an ongoing concern. The 'Capital of Culture' award usually brings with it both pros and cons, with the long-term consequences for former winning cities such as Glasgow cited by both the supporters and the critics of the competition. But in Liverpool's case, the unprecedented privatisation of the city centre will be integral to the changes the city will undergo in the lead-up to 2008, and here in particular the trends are clearly pointing in a worrying direction.

IV. An Inexorable Path?

Despite the picture painted above of growing polarisation, two-speed economies and the demarcation of high-security privatised enclaves, this route ahead for city development is not necessarily an inevitable one.

A comparison of different types of development, and the resulting environments, makes this clear. For example, the regeneration of Bankside in London is universally acclaimed as having genuinely revitalised the riverfront on the south side of the Thames. In contrast, the Millennium Dome, in East London, failed to build on the existing foundations of the surrounding environment, local identity and character of the place, providing instead the feeling of a white elephant plonked on the area, entirely out of context. That it remains an ongoing sore on the government's regeneration record should therefore not come as such a surprise. With its much-mocked corporately sponsored exhibition it has also been seen by many as the ultimate commercial folly, a sign of the millenarian hubris of the New Labour government. The regeneration of Bankside, on the other hand, grew out of the efforts of local community group Coin Street Community Builders and has as its centrepiece the former power station which has long dominated the area, now transformed into Tate Modern.

Both these examples offer key lessons applicable to publicly used spaces in cities. A critical point relates to affordability: the regeneration of Bankside was dependent on the fact that the former Greater London Council leased the land to Coin Street at a subsidised level. Another pivotal issue is the necessity for successful change to work in tune with the character and identity of an area, instead of imposing inappropriate structures, which are unlikely to take root and flourish.

These points and many others relating to cultural identity, diversity and the need to maintain areas of 'free space' will be examined more fully as the project progresses.

Notes

1. This text is based on the initial findings of a longer-term project on the privatisation of public space.

Transformation at Work
Anna Pollert

Back to *Girls, Wives, Factory Lives*

My study *Transformation at Work*[1] concerns the condition of labour in the post-Communist countries of Central Eastern Europe, a decade after the dramatic end of the Cold War. 'Transformation' also has the wider meaning of fundamental change at work, and captures the tone as well as the content of much that has been written over the last two decades about a fundamental change in the nature of capitalist relations. There are many such alleged radical breaks: 'Fordism' to 'post-Fordism', 'industrial' to 'post-industrial', 'material' to 'immaterial' labour, the shift to the 'knowledge economy', the 'informationalisation' of society – in all these, currents in sociological and political literature mirror those in cultural studies of transformations to 'poststructuralism' and 'postmodernity'.

In this exploration of change at work, I shall use my own research, beginning in the early 1970s, as the scaffolding around which to build a more complex picture connecting the nature of workplace change on the ground with wider class relations and the nature of capitalism at the meeting of the twentieth and twenty-first centuries. In summary, this takes me through my early research on class and gender relations in a Bristol tobacco factory, published a decade after the field-work as *Girls, Wives, Factory Lives*,[2] to my critical analysis of radical-break theses around 'Fordism' and 'post-' and 'neo-Fordism' in the 1980s,[3] and finally to European and global relations and post-Communist Europe.

Girls, Wives, Factory Lives can be seen as part of a wider set of 'Bristol studies', alongside those by Nichols and Armstrong and Nichols and Beynon on the lives of ChemCo workers in nearby Avonmouth.[4] These studies took place at the end of the post-war boom, in a period of falling profits, rising unemployment (this reached one million in 1971 when I began my field-work), but also rising industrial militancy. This was the period of the first national dustmen's and building workers' strikes in 1970, the 'work-in' at Upper Clyde shipyards, the miners' strikes and the defeat of the Conservative Party's industrial laws with the 'Pentonville Five' dockers in 1972. Trade union membership was growing, reaching a peak of 55 per cent of workers in 1979. However, the Bristol studies were not about militancy, but about its absence – in what was deemed 'a dozy part of the world'.[5]

Tobacco dominated Bristol, with Wills, the historic company, naming the main university building. The multinational conglomerate Imperial Tobacco, which owned Bristol's tobacco factories in the 1970s, fostered corporate loyalty. Its rhetoric – 'This traditional feeling of belonging to a particular work group is something I want to see strengthened, rather than weakened'[6] – has a familiar ring, chiming with both old paternalism and the allegedly 'new' management of the 1980s and 1990s, appealing to involvement, participation and corporate identity. The reality – rationalisation of jobs, work intensification, relocation and concentration of work in the cheapest and most profitable global sites – is equally familiar. The Churchman's factory in Bristol, where I observed women workers weighing and packing tobacco, rationalised its workforce while I was there, and closed in 1974. By the late 1970s, its ornate Victorian frontage housed small printing firms, and then a shopping arcade – presaging the familiar shift of the 1980s from manufacturing to services, with retail, leisure and cultural industries providing the only employment for the thousands left unemployed after the demise of mining, dock-work and other industries across Britain. Already, the pattern of mine to mining museum, bank to bistro, counter-service bank to call centre, and UK call centre to overseas call centre, was prefigured in the life and death of one factory.

What else was similar then to now? Today's 'human resource management' espouses team working, total quality management, quality circles, briefings, target setting, 'flexibility' and 'constant improvement'. All these were evident, albeit with different labels, in 1971 in Churchman's 'proficiency pay scheme'. Behind the 'flexibility agreement' and policy to 'imbue workers with a sense of responsibility and involvement', worker speed and productivity were monitored electronically, the packing machines set at sixty revolutions per minute, ten empty packs to be filled by each scale every minute, one weighing every six seconds, and anything more than 5 per cent inaccuracies per day a mark on the time sheet, with an eventual pay reduction.

In this period, factory work was relatively well paid compared with other work – which kept the workers (nearly all women) there. However, insecurity and gratitude for having a job were dominant feelings: 'We put up with hard work', 'it's good pay – for women'. In both Churchman's and the mainly male ChemCo, there were dreams of escape into another world: 'When you're young you think you'll stop sometime, and the years slip by. Time flies when you get older, things don't work out like that'. 'We've wasted our lives' (Churchman's worker); 'You're trapped in this job' (ChemCo worker). As for involvement and 'enrichment' (i.e. doing more work for the same pay), as a ChemCo worker said, 'I don't feel enriched, I just feel knackered'.

Fordism, Post-Fordism, Post-Industrialism and 'Radical Break' Theses

Research into the food industry some fifteen years later found that the rhetoric of 'team working' and 'total quality management' was more explicit. This was a period in which it was postulated that a new 'flexible firm' had appeared, in which different workers were either 'numerically' or 'functionally' flexible, and it was also argued that 'Fordist' production had been superseded by a 'post-Fordist' or post-industrial era. What was the empirical evidence for a *new* 'flexible firm', what was the meaning of 'worker flexibility', and what grounds were there for a new paradigm of post-Fordist production?

The 'flexible firm', with a core of relatively secure workers and periphery of expendable workers, was not new. On the contrary, if we look at work patterns in terms of gender, it is clear that for a long time women had been Britain's 'flexible' and disposable workers. What was new was the increased advocacy of such 'flexibility', both by policy makers and in increasingly prescriptive and managerial 'research', leading to secure public-sector employment being increasingly replaced by contracting out and agency work.[7] Since then, there has been an increase in casualisation and precarious work. The alleged break from 'Fordism' to 'post-Fordism' was based on an inaccurate definition of Fordism and the very contestable application of theories of factory management techniques to the quite different context of national economies. The supposed standardisation of Fordist production was set against the 'new' era of constant change and flexibility – but Fordism was already a system based on continual improvement. 'Post-Fordism' was never clearly defined, and its purported flexible and multi-skilled worker was by no means prevalent.[8] The Japanese version, 'Toyotaism',[9] is not an alternative to Fordism, with alleged greater worker flexibility and autonomy; 'it is simply the practice of organisational principles of Fordism under conditions in which management prerogatives are largely unlimited'.[10] As Wood argues, far from superseding Taylorism, just because workers have quality circles does not mean they are not measured and controlled.[11]

'New' production rhetoric had entered the food industry too, but it was clear that the organising principles were an intensified version of those of Churchman's tobacco factory in Bristol over a decade earlier. At Choc-Co, managers were exerting increasingly exacting controls over production workers, as they themselves were more closely financially controlled and evaluated by the 'bottom line' of weekly cost savings in cost centres. The principles of low stocks and just-in-time production, of worker flexibility and involvement, were well entrenched. 'Participation' in so-called 'continuous improvement' and innovation were treated with suspicion, because of insecurity: 'When Thatcherism was in a growth phase, it [the new involvement techniques] was OK. Now, there is fear of a downturn, it's harder to convince people of their role. There's fear of putting forward ideas – it might lose them their overtime'.[12] Research constantly revealed the fact that neither floor managers nor workers were taken in by new inclusive team rhetoric: 'more and more gets pushed down to us – and it's going to get worse', as one team leader put it. Another said, 'Don't call us team leaders, call us mushrooms. Keep 'em in the dark and feed 'em shit'.[13] Much of this echoed the work intensification at Nissan in Washington (Newcastle) and its supply companies,[14] and the experience of workers at Caterpillar who had been offered 'security' for further flexibility, only to be faced with redundancy after corporate restructuring in the late 1980s.[15]

One difference compared to my earlier findings at Churchman's was that these workforces were more divided, between shifts, between part-time and full-time and permanent and agency workers. I questioned whether the 'flexible firm', as this pattern was described, represented security for a 'core' and insecurity for the 'periphery': rather, the evidence was that casualisation and growing insecurity were diffusing throughout organisations, with key workers no more protected than others.

This process accompanied trade union membership decline, which had dropped from its peak of over half the workforce in 1979 to 39 per cent in 1989. This was still a considerable level of organisation compared with 1998, when it had fallen to 30 per cent, and 2001, when it was down to its current 29.1 per cent. This decline in union organisation, while partly due to labour market and sectoral change, was clearly part of Conservative policy, as was the increase in 'management prerogative'.[16] Some of the lines of union resistance witnessed in the 1970s and 1980s, already weak then, are weaker still now (although in the past couple of years a revival has occurred in some sectors). This has implications for the meaning of the 'flexible worker' in the 1980s, and now. As Elger's 1991 review of the survey evidence on management practice in the 1980s showed, much 'flexibility' was aimed at 'greater and/or more continuous effort' and most of it was really about work intensification – again confirmation and strengthening of the management principles of the 1970s, but with much less interference from unions.[17]

Material and Immaterial Labour and Capitalist Diffusion

Given that factories were closing down and work was becoming increasingly service-sector-based (and where material production did continue, the use of information technology was increasing), does this support a 'post-industrialisation' thesis? Is work becoming more informational and immaterial, as is postulated by the now fashionable argument of Hardt and Negri's *Empire*?[18]

To focus on the issue of material versus immaterial labour, if labour is increasingly service-based and 'immaterial', there is little to explain the extreme materiality of a pollution crisis of plastics, refrigerators, cars, mobile phones, and the computers which enable this 'informationalisation'. China is now the rubbish dump for British plastics, Africa and Asia the sites of mountains of poisonous detritus of the electronics revolution.[19] Eighty per cent of the world's manufacturing output is still produced in the US, Western Europe and Japan, and twenty per cent in the Third World. Of course, as productivity increases, fewer workers are needed to do the work. A key feature of the transformation of the capitalist world since the 1980s is the contracting out of work previously done by unionised and relatively well paid workers to those without organisation and on low wages – in Asia, the southern US, and Eastern Europe.

This 'globalisation' is not a decentred global network of information, as Hardt and Negri claim, but the internationalisation of a 'lean production' system[20] – the growth of international production chains organised by transnational corporations, with labour-intensive operations, such as the production of motor parts, printed circuit boards, computer chips and other components, outsourced. In the clothing and shoe industries, cutting and stitching are outsourced, and 'final manufacturers' do the assembling. In financial services, low-waged data processing is outsourced, while more highly paid employees advise corporate clients.[21]

The reality of the capitalist world is that the production of material goods still dominates, with information technology applied to the financial aspect of producing and distributing these goods. But given the internationalisation of material production, can we speak of the growing dominance of 'immaterial labour' in the services of the core capitalist countries, and if this is so, what does it signify? Is this some qualitative break from routinised, Taylorist labour under capitalism? The discourse on 'immaterial labour'[22] refers to 'continual interactive activity' in a wide range of contemporary productive activities, 'transformed labour practices' in the model of information and communication technologies, 'the manipulation of symbols and information' and 'affective labour'. According to Lazzarato, immaterial labour can be seen as the result of a 'great transformation' after the 1970s, when labour entered a period of 'mass intellectuality', with the splits between 'conception and execution, labor and creativity, author and audience' all transcended.[23]

For most workers, however, the qualities of the capitalist labour process dominate. Focusing on one sector of 'immaterial' work – call centres – Taylor and Bain describe 'an assembly-line in the head':[24] repetitive, routinised work, which is intensive, target-driven and stressful, with the additional requirement continuously to perform emotional labour,[25] which frequently leads to 'burn-out'. There is no evidence of a transformation in the capitalist labour process centred on the continuous intensification of wage labour. However, the dystopian view, found in some conceptions of 'immaterial labour', of the complete collapse of collective worker resistance seems unjustified: there is substantial evidence of collective resistance and union organisation, with more than half of call centres in Scotland having a union or staff association in the 1990s.[26]

The 'McDonaldisation' of society[27] spreads standardised and closely monitored work far beyond the archetype of fast food. The process of service sector growth and intensification, standardisation and loss of autonomy confirms Braverman's (1974) elaboration of Marx's analysis of the capitalist labour process. This described how the application of 'scientific management', Taylorism, to the labour process in the 'separation of hand and brain' created 'a variety of new occupations, the hallmark of which is that they are found not in the flow of things but in the flow of paper'.[28] Brown summarises these developments in the capitalist labour process:

> The growing number of 'unproductive workers' inside the enterprise was accompanied by the growth in the number of workers outside the enterprise who were engaged in the 'realisation' rather than the production of surplus value – employees in marketing, advertising, banking, finance, retail and so on. But Braverman argued that these 'new' skills and occupations would undergo the same process of degradation in due course, as the methods of scientific management are applied to the office (and indeed to other service occupations) as well as to the workshop.[29]

Simultaneously, capital expands into other arenas of life, particularly the service industries, transforming domestic work and leisure into commodities. This proliferation of new services is itself subject to the same process of separation of conception and execution.[30] Mandel also explored the reach of capitalism into services, as capital sought to maximise profit wherever it could penetrate.[31]

Nichols, relating his own research at ChemCo to contemporary developments in the nature of work, argues convincingly that the 'transformation' of labour over the past twenty-five years has been characterised not by a radical break, but by the *diffusion* of factory management principles not only to routine service work but also to professional enclaves, such as universities.[32] E.P. Thompson's (1970) revelation of the entanglement of Warwick University with big business[33] was a depressingly accurate presaging of normal practice thirty years later. Not only are chairs financed and named by capitalist companies, and senior posts staffed by ex-managers from big business, but teaching itself is a production process, measured and costed in the same way as a production line, its outputs valued for their contribution to enterprise and business. If courses do not attract markets and income streams, they fail. Similarly, teaching in schools is quantified by league table results and evaluated by the 'value added' to pupils. The privatisation of education in Britain continues apace, with private companies playing an increasing role, and institutions encouraged to compete for market share as their measure of success:

> The [Labour] government's big idea for education turns out to be the one the Conservatives invented 19 years ago, and abandoned as a failure shortly afterwards. It is even run by the same man: Cyril Taylor, the businessman appointed by the Conservatives in 1986 to create 30 city technology colleges. He is now Sir Cyril (apparently because of his services to education) and chairman of the Specialist Colleges Trust. To him fell the honour of trailing in the press the plan to create 200 city academies, on the CTC model, almost a week before it was officially announced. For £2m, less than a fifth of the likely cost, the business owns the school and gets the right to put its name and logo

on it. It gets to decide what specialism the school has and, within the limits of the national curriculum, what subjects are taught. It can even impose its own ideological slant on the teaching.[34]

The same goes for health, with the private finance initiative and foundation hospitals, and the policy is being exported via overseas aid. A recent report by War on Want shows how UK overseas aid is forcing privatisation onto services in developing countries:

> In South Africa, KwaZulu Natal department of health entered into a 15-year public–private partnership for the Inkosi Albert Luthuli hospital in a deal worth $75m in 2001. 'There is now a substantial body of evidence to show that privatisation of public services threatens to expose millions of people in developing countries to increased poverty,' concludes the report. 'Yet the UK government has positioned itself as an international champion of privatisation and DfID channels large sums of the UK aid budget to privatisation consultants.' According to the report, the World Bank is also pressing heavily for a privatisation programme despite the findings of its own internal assessments that it is an area in which 'operations have not paid sufficient attention to the potentially adverse social impact of reforms'.[35]

In all these sectors, management discourse drawn from the factory (targets, output, deliverables, cost centres, performance strategy) or the market (customers) has become 'normal'. These developments are entirely consistent with Marx's analysis and that further elaborated by Braverman in the context of monopoly capital. Current neo-liberal policy oils the wheels of the process.

There is clear evidence from empirical sociology and economics that there has been an inexorable process of intensification of work. This has taken a specific form in OECD countries, in terms of a polarisation between worklessness and increasing work intensity. In Britain, intensification occurs in a number of dimensions. Among those in work, weekly working hours increased from 28 per person per household in 1981 to 31 in 1998. There have also been changes in working patterns, which impinge on welfare. These are associated with the 'flexible labour market' and have meant increases in shift work, weekend working, annualised hours contracts, more bank holiday working and shorter lunch breaks. Britain still evades the European Working Time Directive in including in its 1998 Working Time Regulations the possibility for individuals to opt out of the maximum 48-hour week. The UK pattern of polarisation between increasing numbers working very long hours and increases in those working very short hours continues. Many case studies and interviews with both workers and their managers report higher work pressure and stress.[36]

There is also substantial evidence of increasing job insecurity. By 1994, at least 25 per cent of men and 50 per cent of women in work in the UK held 'non-standard' jobs, such as fixed-term, temporary and agency work. Temporary work has risen, after a period of stability, from 4.1 per cent of total employment in 1991 to the current level of 6.5 per cent. The risk of becoming unemployed has also risen. In 1973–77, 5.6 per cent of British employees experienced a spell of unemployment, a figure which rose to 15 per cent in 1988–1992. What has changed most since the 1970s studies discussed above is that the insecure workforce has spread from manufacturing to services, and in particular to previously privileged professions. In higher education, formal job tenure has ceased, and there is an increase in fixed-term, casual and agency employment. Extensive redundancies have occurred in banking and in local and central government, and globalisation has accelerated the export of jobs overseas.[37]

Transformation at Work: Changes at the End of the Millennium

The diffusion of sophisticated Western management techniques beyond the core zones of capitalism can only be touched on here. Nichols and his colleagues have explored it in factories in East Asia, and observed the spread of attempts at ideological control, but also the neo-liberal-inspired strategy of creating a more 'flexible', insecure workforce.[38] In the context of post-Communist Central Eastern Europe, companies found skilled workers whose wages were one tenth of those in Western Europe. Research in confectionery, brewing, engineering and retail employment found workers with no traditions of trade unionism confronting sophisticated management strategies of intensification and intimidation, together with encouragement of individualism and secrecy.[39] Nevertheless, interviews revealed a very fast learning process among workers: from idealising privatisation and the market, to a suspicion of the 'new' system of capitalism, and resentment at a new form of domination, no longer from the Soviet Union, but now from Western multinationals. Even where overt resistance was lacking (and this is not the case in many countries and several sectors, especially the public sector, where strikes and demonstrations have occurred), then consent and compliance are not evident either.

The experience of workers at the micro-level of the workplace mirrors the subordinate status of Central Eastern Europe in the global economy. Their 'transition' programmes were dominated by the neo-liberal structural adjustment agenda of privatisation, price and trade liberalisation and 'stabilisation' (cuts in public spending) imposed on the 'developing world' by the IMF, the World Bank and the EU. Despite EU enlargement in May 2004, the eight new member states do not have status equal to that of the existing EU-15. And while their workers have long supplied migrant labour to the West, it now transpires that the 'old Europe' has imposed restrictions on the free movement of labour. Only Sweden has refrained. The UK has opened its gates, but while happy for a new Eastern European labour force to work and pay taxes, it refuses to grant social protection (including state health care) for those not in employment. The other countries have imposed a two-year restriction, with Germany retaining the option of extending this to five years.

Conclusions

Both in the UK and across continental Europe, the polarisation between work and worklessness, social inclusion and exclusion, seems to be widening. In Britain, the existence of a Social Exclusion Unit in the Office of the Deputy Prime Minister marks one institutional response to the multiple casualties of free-market capitalism. Recently, the irony and deep symbolism of the Home Secretary's launch of a 'social inclusion' project called 'Positive Futures', based on boxing, seems to have been lost on the government. The initiative reveals an unintended acknowledgment of the violence and frustration bred by the capitalist system, and a cynical willingness to use it as a form of social control. Boxing has long been condemned by the British Medical Association, and its public endorsement in this scheme was severely criticised as likely to cause brain injury to young people. In a telling comment, one fourteen-year-old trainee admitted, 'I know I have a lot of aggression, so I put it into boxing'.[40]

But there is evidence that social control does not succeed in neutralising dissent. Organised resistance is far from dead. As Ronaldo Munck argues, there are increasing examples of trade union resistance and alliances with new social movements, which challenge the inexorable process of globalisation, the search for cheaper labour and work intensification. In one randomly selected issue of *The Guardian* (29 September 2004) I found three examples of worker opposition. P&O Ferries planned to cut 1200 jobs (almost 20 per cent of its workforce) as competition hit the cross-channel ferry business, but the transport union, the RMT, and the officers' union, Numast, refused to rule out industrial action to save jobs, mirroring a bitter dispute in 1988. The HSBC planned to export call-centre jobs abroad, but the union Unifi, which has merged with Amicus, started a high-profile campaign of opposition. Meanwhile, hundreds of British workers who had lost some or all of their pensions planned 'a march and a "Full Monty" striptease' at the Labour Party conference in Brighton.

These examples may suffer similar weaknesses to the struggles of the 1970s, with more bark than bite in many militant-sounding union declarations. They must be seen in a context of union decline and de-collectivisation in Britain. But as the studies of Churchman's and other cases showed, there was no golden age, and it is false to set one up as an idealised past with which to compare the present.

Notes

1. A. Pollert, *Transformation at Work in the New Market Economies of Central Eastern Europe*, London: Sage, 1999.

2. A. Pollert, *Girls, Wives, Factory Lives*, London and Basingstoke: Macmillan, 1981.

3. A. Pollert (ed.), *Farewell to Flexibility?*, Oxford: Blackwell, 1991.

4. See T. Nichols and P. Armstrong, *Workers Divided*, London: Fontana, 1976; T. Nichols and H. Beynon, *Living with Capitalism*, London: Routledge and Kegan Paul, 1977.

5. Nichols and Beynon, *Living with Capitalism*, p. 3.

6. The chairman of Imperial Tobacco in 1979.

7. See A. Pollert, 'The "Flexible Firm": Fixation of Fact?', *Work, Employment and Society*, 2 (1988), pp. 281–316.

8. See A. Pollert, 'Dismantling Flexibility', *Capital and Class*, 34 (1988), pp. 42–75; Pollert (ed.), *Farewell to Flexibility*; K. Williams, T. Cutler, J. Williams and C. Haslam, 'The End of Mass Production?', *Economy and Society*, 16.3 (1987), pp. 405–39.

9. See K. Dohse, U. Jurgens and T. Malsch, 'From "Fordism" to "Toyotaism"? The Social Organisation of the Labor Process in the Japanese Automobile Industry', *Politics and Society*, 14.2 (1985).

10. T. Nichols, 'The Condition of Labour – A Retrospect', *Capital and Class*, 75 (2001), p. 186.

11. S. Wood, 'The Japanisation of Fordism', *Economic and Industrial Democracy*, 14 (1993).

12. Choc-Co manager, quoted in A. Pollert, ' "Team Work" on the Assembly Line: Contradiction and the Dynamics of Union Resilience', in P. Ackers, C. Smith and P. Smith (eds), *The New Workplace and Trade Unionism*, London, Routledge, 1996, p. 194.

13. Quoted in Pollert, ' "Team Work" on the Assembly Line', p. 196.

14. See P. Garrahan and P. Stewart, *The Nissan Enigma*, London: Mansell, 1992; C. Stephenson, 'Trade Unionism in Two Japanese Transplants', in Ackers, Smith and Smith (eds), *The New Workplace and Trade Unionism*.

15. See J. Foster and C. Woolfson, 'Corporate Reconstruction and Business Unionism: The Lessons of Caterpillar and Ford', *New Left Review*, 174 (1989), pp. 51–66.

16. See P. Smith and G. Morton, 'Union Exclusion and the Decollectivization of Industrial Relations in Contemporary Britain', *British Journal of Industrial Relations*, 31.1 (1993), pp. 99–114; W. Brown, S. Deakin and P. Ryan, 'The Effects of British Industrial Relations Legislation 1979–97', *National Institute Economic Review*, 161 (1997), pp. 69–83.

17. See T. Elger, 'Task Flexibility and the Intensification of Labour in UK Manufacturing', in Pollert (ed.), *Farewell to Flexibility*.

18. See M. Hardt and A. Negri, *Empire*, Cambridge, MA: Harvard University Press, 2000.

19. *The Guardian*, 20 and 21 September 2004.

20. See K. Moody, *Workers in a Lean World: Unions in the International Economy*, London: Verso, 1997.

21. See C. Post, review of Hardt and Negri, *Empire*, in *Marxism Mailing List Archive*, archives.econ.utah.edu/archives/marxism/2002w24/msg00030.htm.

22. See M. Lazzarato, 'Towards an Inquiry into Immaterial Labor', *Common Sense*, 22 (2002).

23. Lazzarato, 'Inquiry into Immaterial Labor', p. 1.

24. P. Taylor and P. Bain, ' "An Assembly Line in the Head": Work and Employee Relations in the Call Centre', *Industrial Relations Journal*, 30.2 (1999), pp. 101–17.

25. See A.R. Hochschild, *The Managed Heart*, Berkeley: University of California Press, 1983.

26. Taylor and Bain, ' "An Assembly Line in the Head" ', p. 113.

27. See G. Ritzer, *The McDonaldization of Society*, Berkeley: Sage, 1993.

28. H. Braverman, *Labor and Monopoly Capital*, London: Monthly Review Press, 1984, p. 126.

29. R. Brown, *Understanding Industrial Organisations*, London: Routledge, 1992, p. 186.

30. See Brown, *Understanding Industrial Organisations*, ch. 5.

31. See D. Mandel, *Late Capitalism*, London: New Left Books, 1975; J. Allen, 'Towards a Post-Industrial Economy?', in J. Allen and D. Massey (eds), *Restructuring Britain: The Economy in Question*, London: Sage, 1988.

32. Nichols, 'The Condition of Labour – A Retrospect', p. 190.

33. E.P. Thompson (ed.), *Warwick University Ltd: Industry, Management and the Universities*, Harmondsworth: Penguin, 1970.

34. Francis Beckett, *The Guardian*, 9 July 2004.

35. Duncan Campbell, *The Guardian*, 27 September 2004.

36. See for example F. Green, 'It's Been a Hard Day's Night: The Concentration and Intensification of Work in Late Twentieth Century Britain', *British Journal of Industrial Relations*, 38.1 (2001), pp. 53–81.

37. See E. Heery and J. Salmon, 'The Insecurity Thesis', in idem (eds), *The Insecure Workforce*, London: Routledge, 2000.

38. See T. Nichols, S. Cam, W.G. Chou. W. Zhao and T. Feng, 'Factory Regimes and the Dismantling of Established Labour in Asia: A Review of Cases from Large Manufacturing Plants in China, South Korea and Taiwan', *Work, Employment and Society*, 18.4 (2004), pp. 663–85.

39. See Pollert, *Transformation at Work*.

40. *The Guardian*, 27 September 2004.

41. See R. Munck, *Globalisation and Labour: The New Great Transformation*, London: Zed Books, 2002.

Builders and Warriors, Part II: Walking through Walls[1]
Eyal Weizman

I have long, indeed for years, played with the idea of setting out the sphere of life – bios – graphically on a map. First I envisaged an ordinary map, but now I would incline to a general staff's map of a city centre, if such a thing existed. Doubtless it does not, because of the ignorance of future wars.[2]

Today architectural schools and university urban research institutes promote cities as sites of 'cultural hybridity', 'practical democracy' and 'creative congestion'. At the same time, a series of military urban research institutes and training centres has been set up with the aim of understanding the same categories but to a very different purpose. In fact, according to geographer Simon Marvin, most urban research is currently conducted by men in uniform.[3]

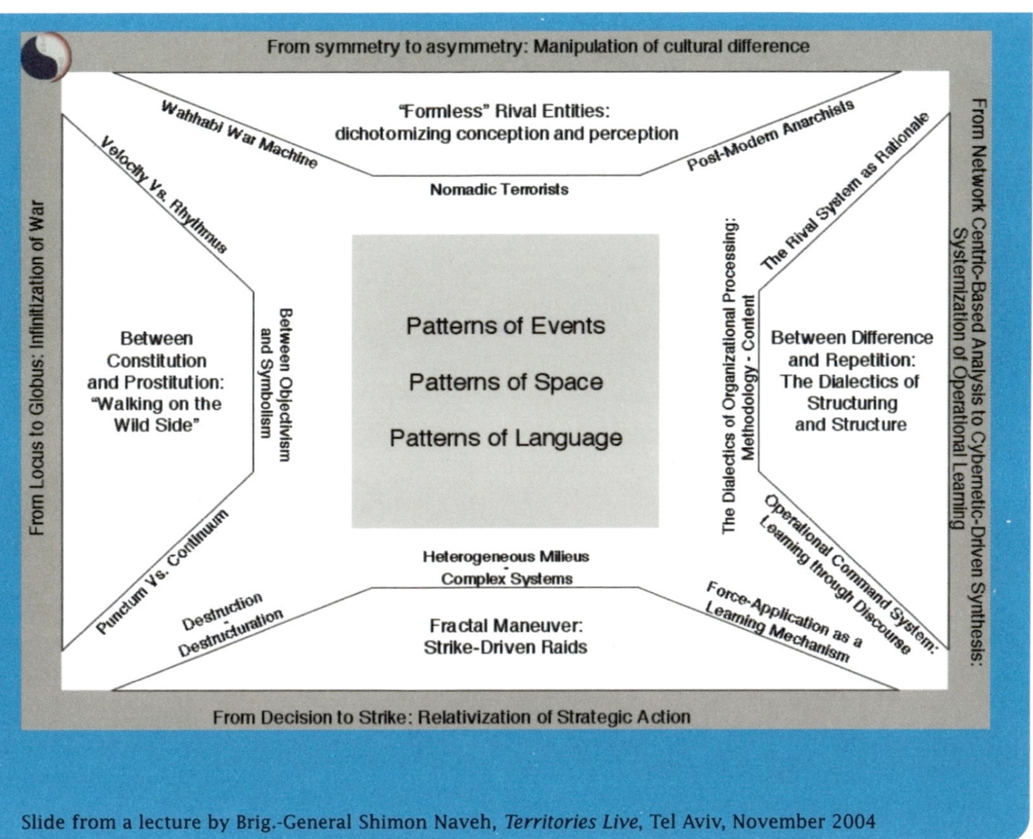

Slide from a lecture by Brig.-General Shimon Naveh, *Territories Live*, Tel Aviv, November 2004

Brigadier-General (ret.) Shimon Naveh is the director of what the Israeli Defence Force calls the 'Operational Theory Research Institute', an institute whose main aim is the basic training of senior military officers in urban and architectural theory. I met him for the first time at a recent conference I co-organised with Anselm Franke as part of the opening of our exhibition *Territories Live* in Israel and Palestine. We wanted to know how and in what terms the military thinks about cities. Naveh's PowerPoint presentation included such headlines as 'Difference and Repetition: The Dialectics of Structuring and Structure', 'Formless Rival Entities: Dichotomising Conception and Perception', 'Velocity versus Rhythms', 'The Wahhabi War Machine: Manipulation of Cultural Difference', 'Post-Modern Anarchists; Nomadic Terrorists', 'Fractal Manoeuvre', and so on. He referred (quite crudely, but all the same) to the work of Deleuze and Guattari, Jean Baudrillard, Jacques Derrida, Paul Virilio, and architects such as Christopher Alexander, Jane Jacobs and Rem Koolhaas. 'We have established a school and we have developed a curriculum that trains operational architects. We develop not only ideas but also methods of work. Our methods of work very much resemble those that architects employ... Can you imagine,' he asked a Tel Aviv audience composed mainly of liberal academics and human rights activists, 'that our soldiers, our generals, are reflecting on this kind of material?'[4] In fact, this very material, which our audience cherished as 'subversive, critical literature', has appeared on military curricula.

Whether Naveh was trying to gain sympathy or respect, he made our audience realise that the way the military sees the city is more complex than we might expect. Simultaneously, the threats the military poses to urban populations, fabric and infrastructure as well as to the very ideal of urban life – as amorphous as this ideal may be – are much greater than we may have imagined. Indeed, the military is rethinking cities and is trying to catch up with their development both in terms of sheer size and numbers and in terms of technological developments, culture and trends. The urban literature that has been so widely produced in the past few decades by writers, architects and academics has become very useful to the military, with soldiers reading anything from 'post-colonial' theory to travel guides and novels about the areas in which they may or actually do fight.

This is How Cities Work

The *Doctrine for Joint Urban Operations*,[5] prepared under the direction of the Chairman of the US Joint Chiefs of Staff, divides cities into three composite parts, which it terms the 'urban triad', in order to 'rationalise' the chaotic complexities a soldier may come across in the urban environment (Marvin reminds us that most soldiers in the US military come from America's rural areas[6]). This includes the physical structure, the infrastructure and the civilian population. This represents a departure from more traditional views of the city, which (up until the peripheral conflicts of the Cold War) described it merely as complex material terrain.

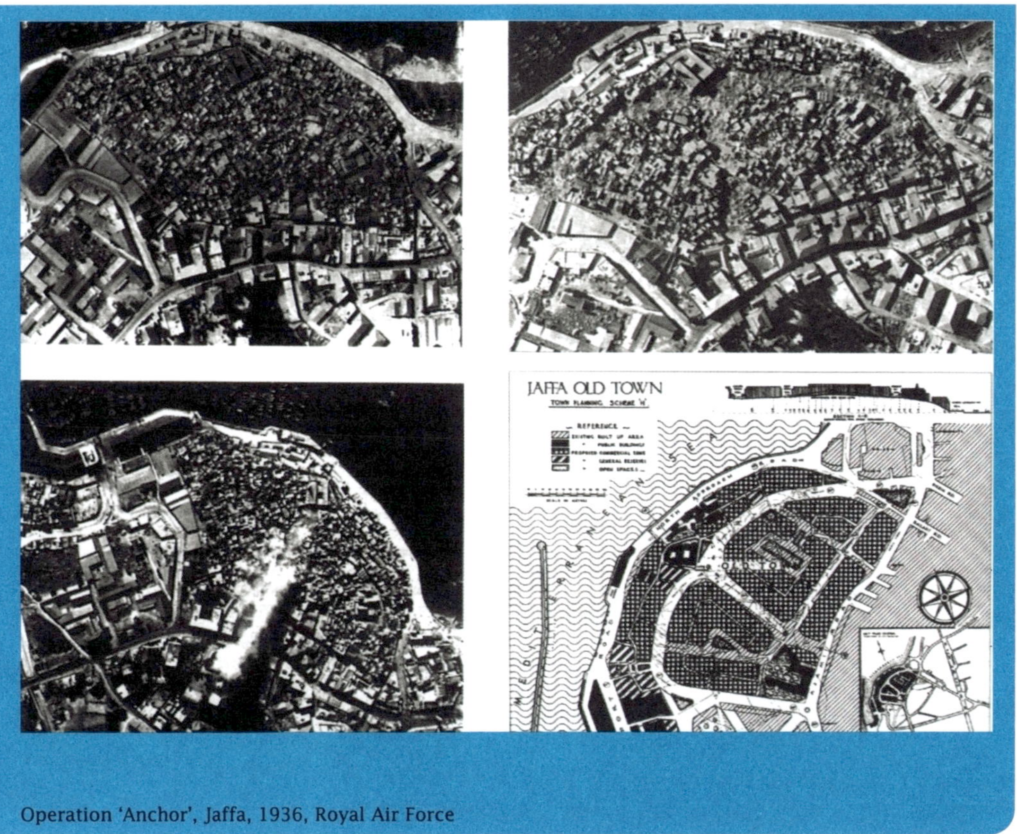

Operation 'Anchor', Jaffa, 1936, Royal Air Force

The **physical structure** refers to buildings and roads, which the military considers the hardware of a city. The forceful reorganisation of physical structure typified urban conflicts of the nineteenth century, and still represents a large component of urban warfare today. 'Design by destruction' implies the shaping of the battle space to suit operational objectives: carving out new roads through dense fabric, the removal of high-rise buildings or other major structures that may provide strategic positions for the enemy or simply stand in the way of what the military defines as its desired path or its essential targets. The view of the city as a complex physical artefact leads to an architectural way of seeing the battlefield (in such terms as 'isolation siege', 'nodal isolation', 'segment and capture', 'soft-point capture and expansion'[7]), by means of which the military abstracts the urban space-time performance.

The second component is urban **infrastructure**. In modern cities with functioning, hierarchical networks of infrastructure, obtaining strategic control of, or being able to activate and deactivate, key networks such as roads, power supplies, water and communications may be more effective than controlling an urban space by military presence. The geographer Stephen Graham claims that with infrastructural warfare whole cities could be switched on and off, causing devastating consequences to their civilian populations.[8] By shutting down electricity and telephone connections in particular parts of a city 'temporarily' (this may in fact imply long periods of time), the military believes it can paralyse its defences or demoralise the urban population into submission. But unlike the planned urban cores, serviced by modern, hierarchical systems of infrastructure, slums and refugee camps present complex non-hierarchical terrains serviced by alternative, informal and non-hierarchical subsystems, present far rarer targets and are far more resilient to attacks. Thus, one may see the Western states' attempts to upgrade infrastructure and living standards in the very places it believes its enemies are 'created' not only as slum clearance operations aimed at the eradication of the breeding conditions for discontent, but also as creating the vulnerabilities that would reduce the motivation of the urban population to support active resistance.[9]

The third component of the city according to the military curriculum is the urban **population**. Through what the US military calls, in Orwellian terms, 'strategies for reprogramming mass consciousness' or Psychological Operations (PSYOP), the urban population is manipulated to act according to the military interest. In its chapter on Psychological Warfare the *Doctrine for Joint Urban Operations* states that

> PSYOP will likely be an integral part of efforts to influence the emotions, motives, objective reasoning, and behaviour of the government, organizations, groups, and individuals in the urban area ... [in order to] positively dispose local officials and non-combatants toward the joint force objectives ... and reduce the morale and effectiveness of enemies and political adversaries ... In the urban environment, the task for PSYOP to get out the [military] approved message is enhanced by the large number of communication devices available to urban residents (cellular phones, facsimile machines, computers, newspapers, radios, televisions, and others).

To facilitate PSYOP, 'cultural intelligence' departments have been set up to uncover the relationship between the social fabric of a city and the built fabric, the logic of social groupings, local politics, and local rivalries – through literature and travel guide books as well as empirical field studies. The aim is to create 'dissidence and disaffection, encouraging defections, promoting resistance, and reducing support among the civilian population'.

'City files' are being compiled in military intelligence archives. In them both existing and newly gathered data – such as maps, aerial images, historical and sociological details, political analysis, and information on dynasties and family connections (in places considered more backward) – is stored. A bank of targets then features places at which attacks could be directed.

The *Doctrine* goes on to discuss how a contemporary urban-military practice can manipulate each of the three components of the 'urban triad'. For this purpose the military employs planners and architects either as external advisers or as military personnel in roles that involve both training and actual plans for reshaping the battle environment to meet political and strategic objectives. Bombing campaigns rely on architects and planners to recommend buildings and infrastructure as targets and in order to evaluate the urban effects of their removal. The destruction in Bosnia of public buildings and spaces – mosques, cemeteries and public squares – followed a clear and old-fashioned planner's logic: social order cannot be maintained without its shared functions. Likewise, the manipulation of key infrastructure (roads, power supplies, water and communications), as undertaken in Ramallah, seeks to control an urban area by disrupting its various flows. The grid of roads that was carved through the fabric of the refugee camp of Jenin and the 'clearing out' of a large area at its centre reveals another planners' speciality, the replacement of an existing circulation system with a system which is more accessible to the occupying army and easier to control popular unrest in. In a strategy often employed by the IDF in the Gaza Strip, earth ramparts were raised to close off areas of operations within a dense urban fabric of homes and streets, providing a temporary architecture of a close perimeter within a part of the city. Indeed, the Israeli army employs architects and civil engineers advising on acts of construction and destruction quite literally as commanders of its destruction bulldozers. The removal of buildings of either tactical or symbolic importance, such as in NATO's 1999 campaign of 'bombing for peace' in Serbia, aims to apply psychological pressure on both the controlling regime and the civilian population. In a revealing article about the NATO bombing strategy in Belgrade the architect and writer Srdjan Jovanovic Weiss claimed that the policy of destruction of buildings 'is also the time of classification'.[10] Choosing targets from a large selection of urban cultural artefacts must include a pretence on the part of the military to understand special cultural and symbolic functions within a matrix of meaning of local cultures, something in which the military has never excelled.

The *Doctrine for Joint Urban Operations* describes these acts, the destruction of homes, schools and roads, as merely 'reshaping the battle-space'. On another occasion US military officer Keith Dickson has defined campaigns of planned destruction as the 're-orientation of the built fabric to create conditions favourable for operational movement and manoeuvre'.[11] Indeed, military jargon is accustoming itself to a cleaner, publicly defensible language in which planning terminology is used to dress up actions which include the levelling of buildings to improve transportation and the destruction of infrastructure to deny water, electricity, and other systems to the defenders – and with them to the entire urban population.

The theoretical investigation of city life and urban culture is complemented by training that provides a simulation of the physical structure of cities. Derelict and depopulated neighbourhoods earmarked for destruction and newly built mock-up cities are prepared for urban training by fun-fair, theme-park or film-set

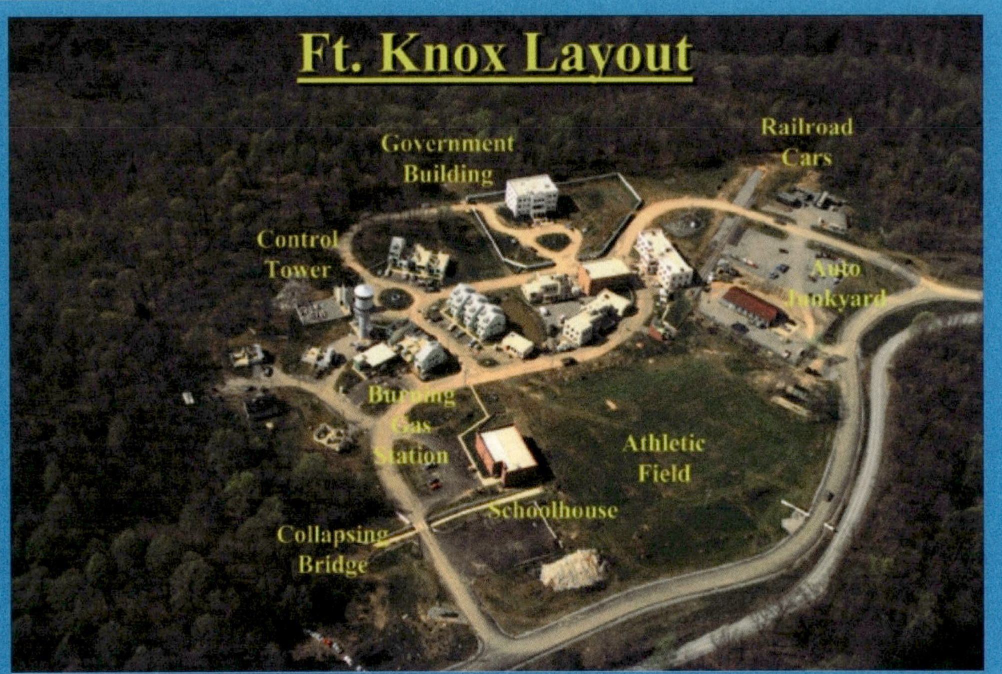

The mock-up city at Ft. Knox, Maine. Core urban warfare training ground.
Seth Bokmeyer, Urban Warfare conference, SMI, London, 2002

architects. Purpose-built mock-up cities are built in such a way that they can be transformed to represent slums of different geographical origin: an African refugee camp, an Arab city, an African metropolis or a Western city in riots or under attack. Action film directors are brought in to help military planners think up possible terrorist scenarios. Soldiers, actors, civilians and sometimes prisoners simulate urban crowds. Special effects and 'cold-fire' systems, recordings of urban life, the sounds of planes, tanks and gunfire and the revolting combination of smells of cooking, decomposing bodies, sewage and stagnant water are released throughout the mock-up cities, allowing militaries a 'taste' of the 'urban mayhem' of refugee camps and urban slums.[12] The US army has increased the number of mock Arab villages from four to 18 and employed Arabic speakers for urban warfare exercises. Hundreds of US military officers have trained in Israel over the last two years in urban warfare and counter-insurgency. The IDF has established several 'academies for urban fighting', one in the Negev desert, where – obscured from view by mountain ridges – the biggest Oriental town since the making of *Ben-Hur* was built, and given the name 'Chicago' in homage to another bullet-riddled town.

But it seems that the most effective exercise in contemporary urban warfare was Operation 'Defensive Shield', which has become the most important reference point for the doctrine of urban warfare.

Operation 'Defensive Shield'

On 29 March 2002 the IDF launched Operation 'Defensive Shield', an offensive whose stated aim was the dismantling of the only thing that the political and military establishments imagined as able to be dismantled, an imaginary 'infrastructure of terror' that does not register the popular support for acts of resistance, but the social and physical structures that allowed for a series of suicide bombings within Israeli cities.[12] Stephen Graham recounts the way in which, in the months preceding the attacks of 'Defensive Shield', refugee camps were no longer portrayed as places of habitation for displaced people, but dehumanised as 'terrorist nests' or naturalised as an 'urban "cancer", that undermines the order, progress, and existence of the purported organic "body" of the modern State of Israel'. Graham quotes the words of Efi Eitam – one of Israel's

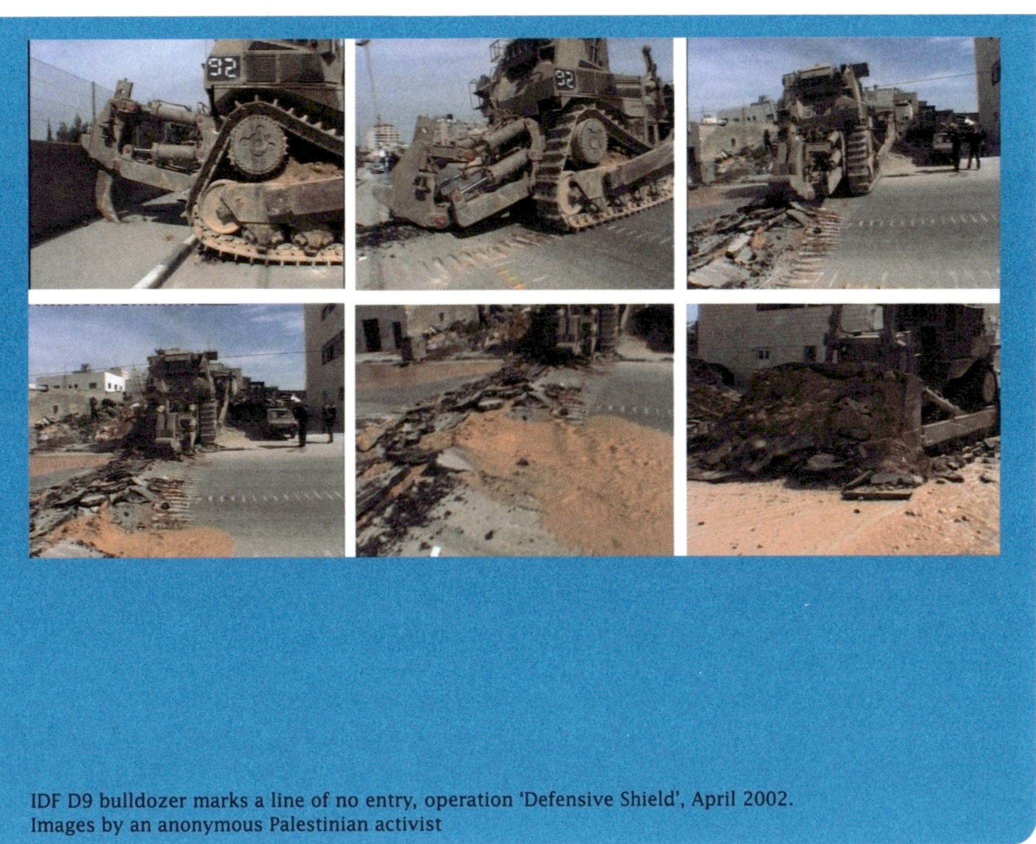

IDF D9 bulldozer marks a line of no entry, operation 'Defensive Shield', April 2002.
Images by an anonymous Palestinian activist

most radical national-religious leaders – who described the camps as 'a human, demographic and social time bomb waiting to "explode" upon the Israeli state'.[14]

Although the operation was played out within Palestinian urban environments with different characteristics – a modern city in Ramallah, a dense historic city centre at the Kasbah of Nablus, an international holy city in Bethlehem and refugee camps in Jenin, Balata and Tul-Karem – they were all projected in the simplified imaginary cartography of the Israeli media as evil, strange and dangerous places, or as 'essentially unknowable, closed and un-occupy-able spaces'.[15] Brigadier-General Aviv Kokhavi, who commanded the paratrooper brigade in the battle of Balata refugee camp and the Kasbah, stated that '[there] is no doubt about the psychological dimension of entering a refugee camp. Even the very words "refugee camps" themselves are strong enough to bring out a negative aura ... All that is even more true since for many years no military action was carried out there, and thus together with the mosques hollering "Balata will be the mother of all resistance" ... a feeling that something very big was about to happen was created'.[16]

The offensive began with isolating all cities, towns and refugee camps that were about to be attacked, and cordoning them off with barbed wire ditches and dykes into a series of 'closed-off military zones'. All entry and exit roads were cut off and full curfew was imposed within them. The inhabitants were locked within what effectively became a series of urban death-traps.

Balata is similar to Jenin in that they are both small refugee camps on the outer margins of a Palestinian city. Both were avoided by the IDF for many years and were seen as impenetrable and thus as extraterritorial enclaves. IDF operations in both camps were to have similar objectives: to kill or arrest members of the Palestinian resistance and to intimidate the rest of the population to prevent them assisting the 'rebels'.

After the operation in Jenin and in response to the negative effects of the publicity the military received, the IDF felt it necessary to provide further courses for its engineer corps soldiers, as well as for architects and engineers on IDF reserve duty, to improve their art of demolition (Haussmann called himself a demolition artist). At a recent military conference, an Israeli engineering officer specialising in the destruction of Palestinian homes mentioned to his international audience that, 'helped by the study of building, construction and structures', 'the military can remove one floor in a building without destroying it completely or remove a building that stands in a row of buildings without damaging the others'.[17] With its increasing perfection of the ability to destroy, the military is better able to redesign the 'habitat of terror' according to its needs.

Urbicide

The destruction of homes does not merely relate to the Israeli strategic objective of limiting Palestinian urban growth (although it forms a large part of it), quantified as a statistical problem relating to numbers of destroyed buildings, but must be understood as an active form of design having a cumulative effect in the creation of new spaces. International law, largely drafted in the first half of the twentieth century, is inadequate to deal with present violations associated with the emergent urban strategies of contemporary conflicts. Predicated on a clear dialectics of 'war' and 'peace', 'civilians' and 'combatants', its imaginative horizon still relates to urban warfare as practised in the (more or less) symmetrical engagements of the World Wars, and relates in too limited a manner to civilians living in those cities. The relevant War Crimes articles dealing with urban destruction forbid '[e]xtensive destruction and appropriation of property … carried out … wantonly' (Rome Statute Article 8.2.a.iv),[18] and '[i]ntentionally directing attacks against buildings dedicated to religion, education, art, science or charitable purposes, historic monuments, hospitals and places where the sick and wounded are collected' (Article 8.3.b.ix),[19] but only so long as these categories do not contain buildings that are being used as cover or refuge by the enemy.

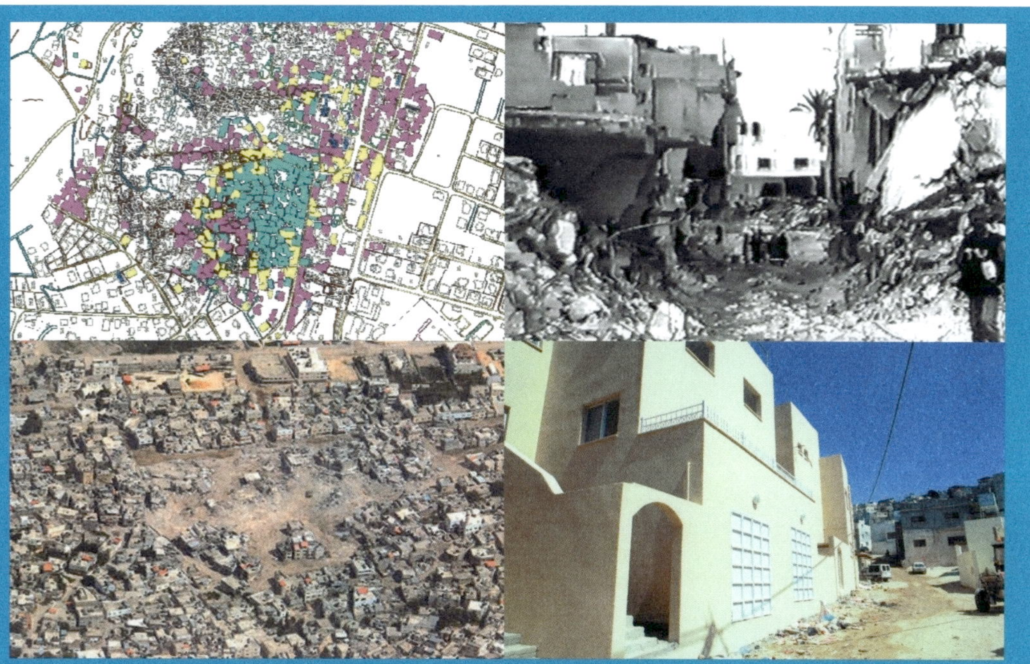

Jenin refugee camp after the battle of April 2002
Blue squares denote completely demolished buildings
Red squares denote partially damaged buildings

Jenin refugee camp, Israeli Air Force, April 2002

New route cut through the urban fabric of Jenin refugee camp. Image by anonymous Palestinian activist, April 2002

New homes built by UNRWA to replace the destroyed homes in Jenin refugee camp. Miki Kratsma, June 2004

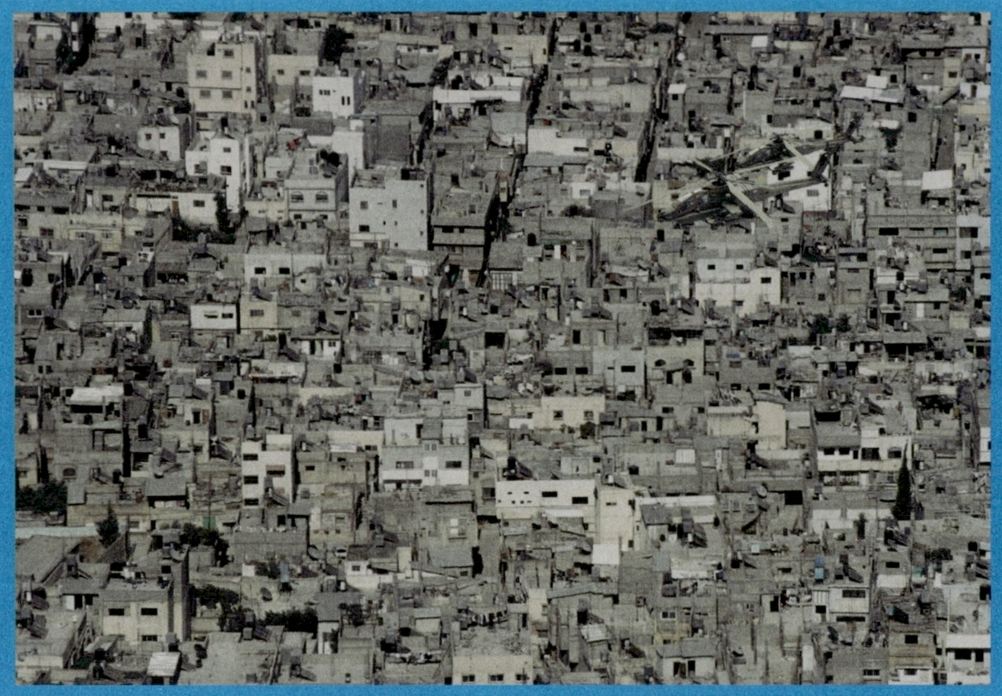

The refugee camp of Balata, Nablus, Nir Kafri, 2003.
In the battle of April 2002 80 Palestinians were killed in this camp.

International humanitarian law forbids either the complete destruction of cities, large parts thereof, or the destruction of specific public buildings within them. Although the IDF was never required to answer for its operation in Jenin in terms of international law, if it did have to, it might be able to argue that, according to the present formulation of the law, the buildings targeted were largely private homes and not public buildings. Moreover, the military could have claimed that their destruction was a military necessity. The semantics of international law are still inadequate to describe this battle; future reformulations of international humanitarian law may find a way to classify the destruction of the refugee camp of Jenin as a war crime for its very acts of 'design by destruction', the reorganisation of the urban habitat, and the attack on urbanity itself.

The fact that the logic of 'design by destruction' was carried through to the reconstruction of the camp is well demonstrated by a conflict that erupted between the residents of the camp and its planners concerning its urban design. Funds received from the United Arab Emirates totalling US$26 million dollars allowed UNRWA (the United Nations Relief and Works Agency) to implement a new master-plan for the camp and replace most of the homes destroyed during the operation with new buildings. Under the path of destruction, new sewage and

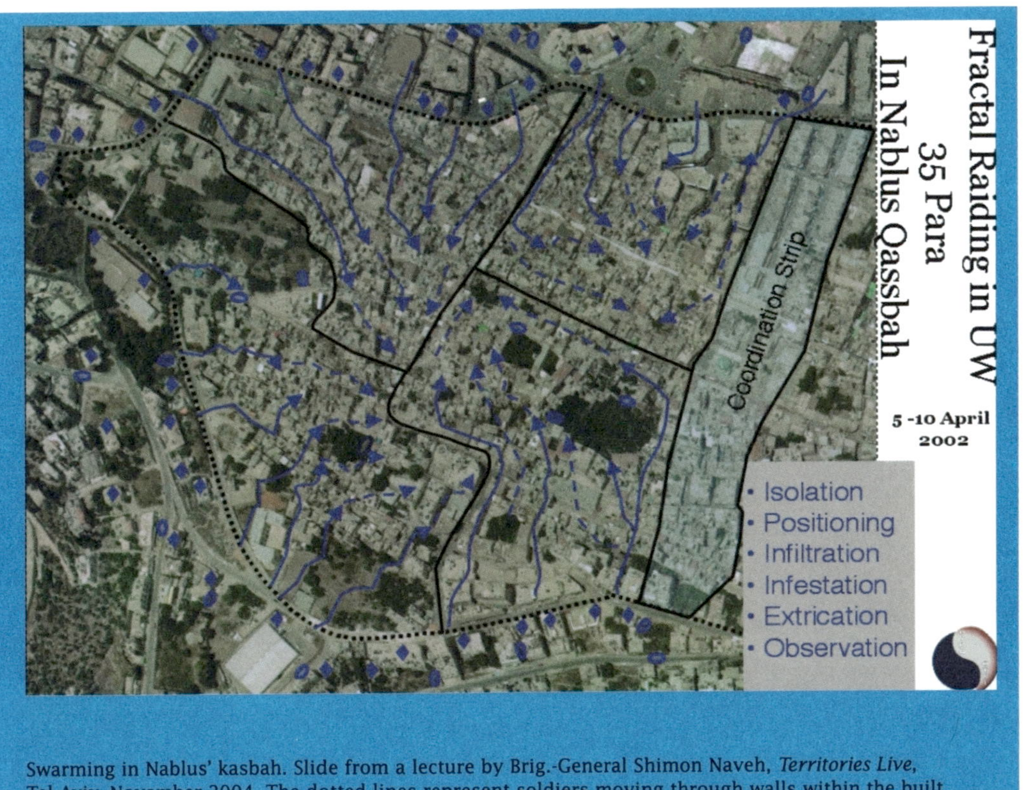

Swarming in Nablus' kasbah. Slide from a lecture by Brig.-General Shimon Naveh, *Territories Live*, Tel Aviv, November 2004. The dotted lines represent soldiers moving through walls within the built fabric of the city.

water systems were to be laid out. After much debate and in the face of strong protests by the popular committees, in which the resistance is well represented, UNRWA decided to allocate some 15 per cent of the original size of the ground-plans of destroyed homes to widen the roads of the camp in a way that would allow Israeli tanks to access the camp in the future without having to break through the walls of homes! Representatives of the armed organisations opposed having their homes and streets designed according to the standard width of an Israeli tank, stating that 'it should be made more, not less difficult for Israeli tanks to enter the camp',[20] but the camp's political committee decided to widen the roads, mentioning other benefits – such as improved traffic flow and services – to support their aim.[21] In some areas it was only the ground floor that was pushed back – less than a metre on each side of the road – with the rest of the building overhanging this space. The space taken from private homes was compensated for by allowing the structures to be extended vertically or by alternative space allocated for construction at the outskirts of the camp. In a related dispute, some Islamic organisations demanded that the walls separating the streets from the private spaces of the homes be lowered so that passers-by could monitor the modesty of women inside.

Swarming

In March and April 2004 the developments of the battles of Balata and Nablus were the focus of a conference on 'limited conflict', attended by military officers from 35 countries. Besides the obvious presence of the US, UK, Russia and Australia, delegates also attended from China, Brazil, Singapore, Jordan, Poland, France, Germany and the Czech Republic – countries that would generally condemn Israeli military actions on every political stage, but now sent delegates to Israel to be inspired by Israeli urban warfare experiences.

Arguably the most important presentation was by Brigadier-General Aviv Kokhavi. According to Kokhavi the operation in Balata and Nablus was conducted as a simultaneous approach of small semi-autonomous units from all directions. From the enemy's perspective, soldiers appear everywhere, moving through alleys, cracks, walls, and then pull out as fast as they came in. At each location the military, adopting the tactics of guerrilla warfare, would, according to Kokhavi, 'stealthily enter from several directions, fire four bullets here, 10 there ... and move to another position before being spotted'. In this form of battle, the military adapt guerrilla tactics. 'Sometimes limited amount of fire can cause total chaos and disorientation for the enemy ... which would not quite know where it is being attacked from', he told his audience of soldiers.

According to the military historian Yagil Henkin, the tactic implemented by the IDF in the battle of Nablus is 'swarming' – the new buzz-word in the doctrine of RMA (Revolution in Military Affairs)[22] emerging from the post-Cold War US armed forces. In contrast to a linear operation, in which military columns progress gradually from the outside in, securing the axis as they move on, 'swarming' through the urban environment seeks to organise attacks from the inside out, changing directions constantly, so defenders may find it hard to predict the attacker's next move. In theory a 'swarming' force 'has no form, no front, back or flanks, but moves like a cloud' and should be measured by location, velocity and density, rather then power and mass. Another enthusiastic military journalist likened this 'new' tactic to 'an octopus that attacks along the depth and across the width of the fields of operation'.[23]

Vasily Ivanovich Chuikov, who was in command of the 62nd Red Army at the Battle of Stalingrad, created the model for what militaries later referred to as 'swarming' in urban warfare. Unable to control the entire battle and pockets of Red Army resistance scattered through Stalingrad, Chuikov gave up centralised and direct control of his army, breaking its rigid formation into a large number of small semi-independent units. The urban battle no longer consisted of a single linear operation, but fragmented into simultaneous series of repetitive engagements. The result was an emergent behaviour that repeated its patterns on various scales, where the interaction between the independent units created what the military now calls a 'complex adaptive system', making the total effect of the units' actions larger than the sum of their components.[24]

While the traditional military strategies are linear in the sense that they follow a pre-determined consequential sequence of operations, a cascading flow of events in which present actions allow future ones to be performed and add up to a complete battle plan, warfare in the urban environment,[25] just like cities themselves, is complex, simultaneous, unexpected and non-linear. Although in the urban battle-space actions are deterministic, they are highly sensitive to minute irregularities, in a way that interferes with the ability of the military to form its battle plans and keep them coherent. The single-track narrative of the clockwork-like linear battle is therefore replaced with the non-sequential and simultaneous approach of the 'toolbox'. The toolbox doctrine means that soldiers and officers learn how to deal with emergent situations and receive the appropriate tools (weapons, ammunitions or devices) to deal with them, but since they cannot predict the order in which these events may occur, the military retains the flexibility to fight without a prescribed sequential plan. By dematerialising itself from a heavy, linear 'geometrical' system and reassembling itself as a loose and dynamic organisation, the military attempts to use the chaos and the non-linearity of the urban environment to its advantage.

Where the traditional strategy of urban warfare seeks, in the 'shaping of the battlefield', to subject cities such as Algiers, Jaffa, Paris or Jenin to its utilitarian military logic of transportation, communication and visual control, in employing the 'swarming' tactics the military attempts to adapt itself to the complex nature of cities. To a large extent, the 'swarming' tactic is nothing but a formalised military version of 'classic' urban guerrilla tactics. The defenders of the Paris Commune, much like those of the Kasbah of Algiers, Stalingrad, Hue, Beirut, Jenin and Nablus, navigated the city through openings and connections between homes, basements and courtyards, through alternative routes, secret passages and trap-doors. In the early years of the last century, the second stage of Mao's liberation war promoted coordinated guerrilla action, complete with well-timed concentrated attacks, camouflaging tactics, and deep penetration, replacing linearity with simultaneity.[26]

For Manuel DeLanda the process by which militaries gradually replaced cohesion with dispersed synergy is the history of modern warfare itself. He describes the way in which the cohesive, hierarchical, clockwork-like armies of the sixteenth century controlled, by rigidly imposed collective routines, every motion needed to load, aim and fire a musket, turning the military into a man-machine apparatus that increased collective efficiency but reduced the control that each individual soldier had over his own actions. Standing in two interchangeable rows, the forward one firing and the backward one loading, these armies were controlled by the cascading chain of command down to the smallest movements and actions of the individual. DeLanda describes the Blitzkrieg armies of the Second World War as relatively decentralised organisations, in which military units on the move operated with considerable leeway for independent actions. 'By lowering the thresholds of decision-making through the authorization of more local initiative,'

DeLanda writes, 'different parts of the machine can deal with a small amount of uncertainty. ... mission oriented tactics,[27] in which only the outlines and the overall goal of an operation are laid down ... adapt fluidity, dispersing friction and allowing transient events to "invoke" procedures and capabilities'.[28]

This command system relies on increasing the freedom for making decisions on the immediate tactical level to provide an answer to rapidly developing situations. The high level of performance of von Moltke's armies on the Eastern Front was thus enabled by the readiness of the higher command to accept more uncertainty at its own headquarters while reducing uncertainty at the lower tactical level. This allowed local situations to be resolved by local initiative – minimising the broken communications that inevitably occur along the long chain of command of rigidly hierarchical, top-down operations. Decentralised operations are in effect complex self-organising systems whose patterns replicate themselves like fractals on every scale.

By limiting visibility and manoeuvrability, the urban terrain breaks up large military formations into small units. In a swarming manoeuvre, synergy between highly dispersed semi-autonomous units is thus seen as a force multiplier.

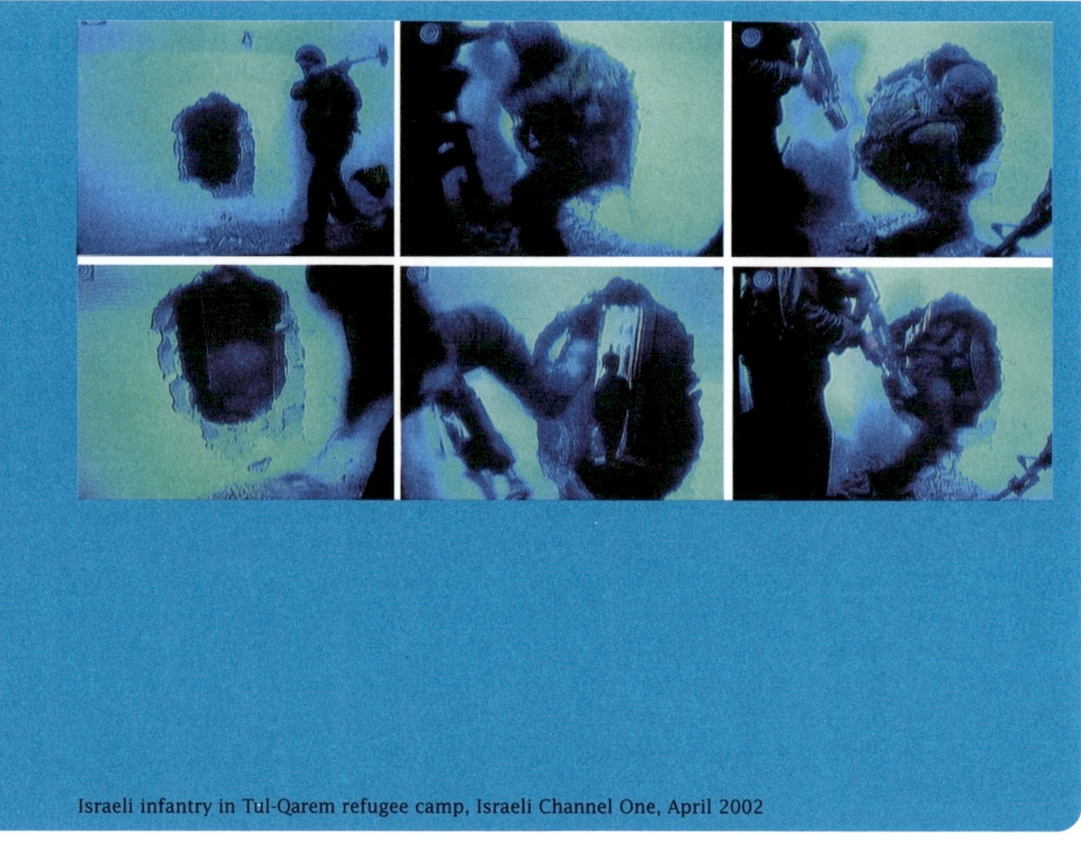

Israeli infantry in Tul-Qarem refugee camp, Israeli Channel One, April 2002

According to the US military RMA term 'Network-Centric Warfare', this synergy requires the networking of all friendly forces across the battlefield into a single information-sharing system. The vision is that the synergetic integration of air and ground forces would allow every unit commander to receive information from all available sources. 'Cross vision' means joining several perspectives – that of the infantry soldier on the ground and that of the pilot – into a newly composed battle image. In contrast to non-networked swarming operations, this allows the disparate units to rejoin into nodes networked within a single coherent organisation. Beyond the fact that in contemporary urban battlefields almost all soldiers are already connected through a private radio system to their commanders and fellow soldiers, future innovations seek to give each soldier access to real-time reconnaissance, intelligence and video imaging, as well as to register his position within the battlefield. The aim is to plot the overlapping movements of soldiers in terms of their X, Y coordinates on the plane (or their 'address') and the Z coordinates for their latitude (or the 'floor') across the urban fabric on three-dimensional, hologrammatic cartography in real time at central headquarters.

While these innovations are still on the drawing board, urban navigation during Operation 'Defensive Shield' was conducted on aerial maps on which each Palestinian home and building had been abstracted into a catalogue number. Some Israeli soldiers used their personal hand-held mobile phones to communicate with tank commanders and among themselves in order to coordinate operations.[29] Similarly, Chechen fighters in Grozny coordinated attacks on Russian troops with Russian networked mobile phones. Palestinian fighters used mobile phones during battle to coordinate the defence of the camp, until they realised that an open hand-held phone transmits radiation that gives away its location and may be followed by a GPS-guided bomb.

Helicopters, unmanned aerial vehicles and unmanned balloons were positioned above the battlefield day and night to deliver constant live updates about the constantly transforming battlefield. At night, the camps of Jenin and Balata were so strongly lit with projectors and light-bombs that the two-week-long operation turned the camps into non-space-time bubbles.

Walking Through Walls

Swarming requires an ability to move fast and unexpectedly across all dimensions of the city. What Kokhavi referred to in the military conference as 'inverse geometry' is in effect a reorganisation of the urban syntax by a series of micro-tactical actions. In contrast to the operation conducted in Jenin, which ended up with the erasure of an entire neighbourhood, the reorganisation of the Balata camp and later of the Kasbah of Nablus were not conducted on the scale of the military vehicle – the bulldozer or the tank – and thus did not necessitate the

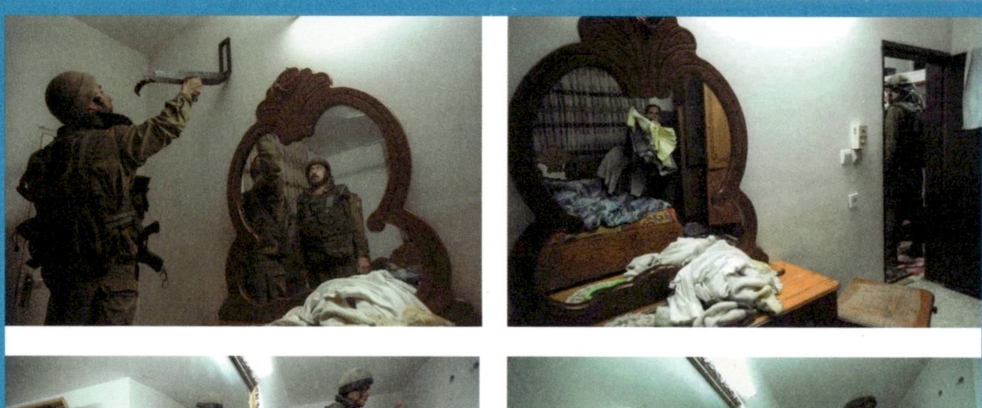

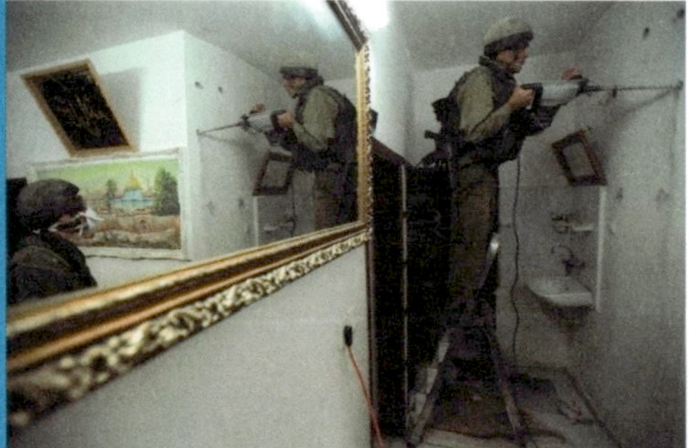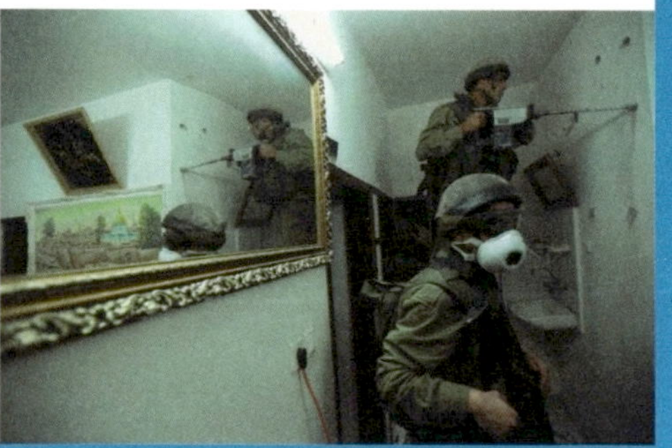

Israeli engineers in Tul-Qarem refugee camp, Nir Kafri, 2003

breaking of new roads. However, the level of the infantry soldier and the scale of the home brought the path of destruction to the interior space of many Palestinian homes. Soldiers moved across the depth of the camp by cutting new routes through the walls that separated adjacent structures. Breaking unexpectedly into the private space of inhabited homes, they were essentially tunnelling their way, sometimes hundred of metres, through the urban fabric. Movement between buildings took place most often on the second floor of buildings because the ground floor and the doorways were booby-trapped. Absorbed by the walls on one side of the camp, soldiers came pouring out of cracks and fissures in different points deep within it.

In an interview conducted by Nadav Harel, Anselm Franke and myself with Aviv Kokhavi in September 2004, Kokhavi said:

> Our think tank has decided ... to simply look at space [as] architecturally different ... meaning not to obey the alleys, that were planned by whoever planned them or that evolved as they did – because even in urban design one plans one thing but something quite different may turn out – but we meant to interpret the urban space in a different fashion.

This room that you see is nothing but your *interpretation*, and you can stretch
your interpretation within the limits of architecture and physics. Similarly the
alley could be interpreted, as any architect and urban planner does, as a place
to walk through, but it could as well be interpreted as a place which is
forbidden to walk through. That is only interpretation. We interpreted the alley
as a place forbidden to walk through, and the door as a place forbidden to pass
through, and the window as a place forbidden to go through, because a weapon
awaits us in the alley, and a booby trap awaits us behind the doors. Because the
enemy interprets space in a traditional, classical manner, and I do not wish to
obey this interpretation and fall into his traps. Not only do I not want to fall
into his traps, I want to surprise him. This is the essence of war. I need to
emerge out of an unexpected place, and this is what we tried to do. This is the
reason that we opted for the method of moving through walls. In many places
through small holes [that we blasted], similar to a worm cutting through as it
eats its way onwards – sometimes appearing outside and then disappearing. We
were thus moving from the interior of homes to their exterior in an unexpected
manner and in places where we were not expected, arriving behind and hitting
the enemy that awaited us behind a corner. Because it was the first time that
this method was performed [on such a scale], we were learning through action,
how to adjust ourselves to the relevant urban space, and similarly how to
adjust the relevant urban space to our needs. We took this micro-tactical
practice [of moving through walls] and turned it into a method, and because of
this method we were able to interpret space differently! I informed our soldiers
– friends! – This is not for your consideration! – There is no way of moving
otherwise! – If until now you were accustomed to move in the city along roads
and sidewalks, from now on we all walk through walls!

In the contemporary urban battlefield 'worming' has gradually become the
indispensable material counterpart of 'swarming'. As a physical transformation
and material reorganisation of city syntax, it is performed to allow for free, three-
dimensional movement through the solid fabric of the city. In the early stages of
the battle of Jenin, as well as during the entire battle of Nablus, both soldiers and
the Palestinian defenders tunnelled through the city's fabric, often crossing each
other's routes at a few metres' distance.

Sharon Rotbard argues that 'worming', just like the carving out of new roads
through alienated cities, was invented and 'publicised' in every period anew, out
of the tactical necessities of urban war, without its 'inventor' being aware of the
previous occasions on which it had been practised. According to Rotbard, the first
time this tactical movement through the city is recorded is in Marshal Thomas
Bugeaud's *La Guerre des Rues et des Maisons*, in the context of anti-insurgency
tactics in the class-based urban battles of Industrial Revolution-era Paris.[30]
Although different, the built fabric of nineteenth-century Paris and that of
Palestinian refugee camps share at least two characteristics: they were both
inhabited by poor populations in low quality homes and had buildings densely

packed together. Both urban areas were seen as sites of danger and talked about as unhygienic, contaminated and contaminating to the body politics of the states they were in.

Deeply ingrained in Zionist urban war-making is the way in which the geography of the Palestinian city (and later the refugee camp) is imagined. Such cities and camps are often seen as nothing but pre-modern, formless, almost solid conglomerates of material and human refuse – treacherous, dangerous places that could only be subdued through the simplification and hygienic practices embodied by the act of 'design by destruction'. 'Free' paths were to be carved through the 'formless' masses of Palestinian cities and camps by generations of Zionist 'builders and warriors'.

It is thus not surprising that 'worming' has become almost the only way in which military men would enter a Palestinian home. The assassination squads of Lieutenant-Colonel Eyal Weiss, commander of the undercover Arabist 'Duvdevan' ('cherry') unit – whose soldiers are dressed as Arab civilians[31] – never entered buildings through the doors where they were sometimes expected, but blasted in through openings at the back or side or through much longer 'over-ground tunnels' drilled through neighbouring buildings. It is ironic that Weiss himself was killed in February 2002 when a wall collapsed and buried him during an 'operation' in a West Bank village.

Considering the fact that about 80 per cent of military casualties routinely occur outside buildings, the military sees 'worming' as a way to protect the lives of its own soldiers at the expense of civilian lives and property. In case anyone imagines that soldiers moving through walls has only minor consequences, the following is a description of the sequence of events. Soldiers quietly assemble behind a wall, stick explosive charges on it or break a hole with a large hammer. The charge through the open hole is usually preceded by stun grenades and a few random shots into what is most often the private living room of an unsuspecting family. The stunned residents – often families of more than fifteen people – are assembled and locked within one of the rooms, where they may be made to remain, sometimes for several days until the battle ends, often without water, toilets, food or medicine. And so on into the next home. It is not hard to imagine the consequences of these acts for lives and property. Soldiers moving through evacuated living rooms often help themselves (although looting is closely monitored by the IDF) to whatever is small enough to fit into their pockets, and sometimes use the contents otherwise for their own needs. If moving through walls is often pitched by the military as its 'humane' answer to the cruelty of urban warfare, this is because the damage it causes is often concealed within the interiors of homes.

The wall, usually seen as the last barrier to privacy – perhaps the last absolute given of architecture – is slowly evaporating. The development of instruments with the ability to see through walls and therefore to render architecture transparent is defined by the military as indispensable, the absolute prerequisite of all future urban warfare. Based on technology that resembles ultrasound, wall surveillance radar systems are being designed to provide high-resolution three-dimensional renderings of entire rooms located behind solid walls.[32] Special ammunition for personal rifles capable of piercing reinforced concrete walls without deflecting is being developed, to complement the ability to see with the ability to kill.

It is interesting to note that the US military has employed Israeli urban warfare tactics. US officers were present on the West Bank during the last days of Operation 'Defensive Shield' and, especially around Balata, Nablus and the Jenin refugee camp, inspected the battlefield incognito wearing IDF uniforms.[33] Hundreds of US marine corps officers have trained in Israel over the last two years in urban warfare, targeted assassinations, and in what the military crudely calls 'population management' – a term wide enough to include everything from an extended policy of curfews and blockades to management of the civil affairs of the occupied population by an occupying army.

Urban Frontiers

Acts of 'design by destruction' grow out of the perception that in urban warfare, fighting is not merely an action that takes place within a city: rather, the city, a complex terrain and 'impenetrable' obstacle as it may be, is not merely the location of war, but is its very weapons and means. Through a process of appropriation, adaptation, interpretation and destruction it becomes the medium by whose transformation the battle takes shape.

Graham has claimed that the battle over the refugee camps in Palestine amounts to 'urbicide' – a term coined by Marshal Berman in relation to the destruction of the Bronx during the intense and brutal urban regeneration programmes of the 1960s.[34] Graham refers to the destruction of the urban as an act of murder directed against the physical fabric and against the very idea of a city, its conditions of heterogeneity, plurality and congestion.[35] By directly assaulting the very 'messiness' and 'anarchic' heterogeneity that a dense urban fabric inevitably produces, urban operations often present themselves as hygienic acts of 'disinfection'.

The destruction of the Arab city or the refugee camps includes yet another dimension. The oriental city has been produced in the Western cultural imagination as a site different and strange, full of deceit and dangers – a place whose uncontrolled material and demographic growth threatens our modern home-cities and way of life. Graham has traced that attitude in the Israeli political-military elite, who refer to the spontaneous construction of Palestinian housing and refugee camps as the 'Jihad of buildings'[36] – a war in which the

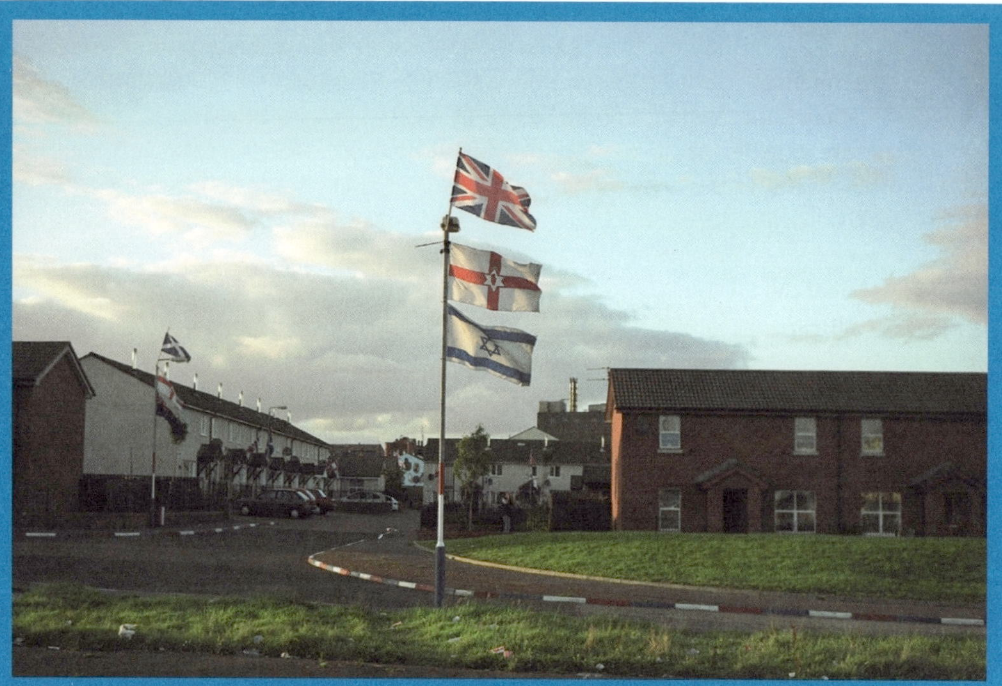

Flags in Belfast. Israeli flags are often used by unionists whereas Palestinian flags are used by republicans, reproducing the Israeli/Palestinian conflict within Northern Ireland. Photograph: Scott Hopkins, 2002

urbanisation of the terrain is the battlefield, and within which the uncontrolled, spontaneous and 'illegal' sprawl constructs the buildings as a weapon.

This constructed difference, in Israel, Palestine and elsewhere, is the reason that Western soldiers and the constituencies that allow them to operate accept that forceful interference, targeting and destruction are unavoidable, natural and necessary responses that are capable of *reforming a backward enemy* – in as much as they rework and take away his conditions of dissatisfaction.

The military methods used in the operations in Jenin and in Balata cover much of the spectrum of military operations in urban terrain. If the first attempted, with its old-fashioned notion of 'design by destruction', to reorganise an urban fabric in a way that suits military needs, the second attempted to adapt itself to the complexities of the urban environment in becoming something of the guerrilla forces it was sent to destroy. Both methods cause considerable destruction and death, and breach international and human rights law. Because innovations in military action tend to be followed by a process of 'civilianisation', the above-mentioned operations may become relevant to the future conditions of our cities. 'Civilianisation' implies not only the migration of technologies, methods and concepts from the military to the civilian domain, but also geographical transfer, the spread of violence from the periphery (where extreme methods are experimented with) to the centre (where they are most effective), and vice versa. If we have understood the tale of the two camps as a laboratory for future acts of warfare exported from Palestine, further east to Iraq, Afghanistan and other such present or future fringes of an angry imperial order, the present condition of permanent low-level conflict makes urban warfare, crime and riot control no longer easily distinguishable, and may reinforce the policies and tactics of 'national defence' in relation to the 'Balatas' and 'Jenins' that already exist within our cities.

Notes

1. This is the second part of a two-part work; the first part was published in *Site* magazine, Sweden, in November 2004.

2. Walter Benjamin, *One-Way Street and Other Writings*, London: Verso, 1979, p. 295.

3. Simon Marvin, 'Military Urban Research Programmes: Normalising the Remote Control of Cities', paper delivered at 'Cities as Strategic Sites: Militarisation, Anti-Globalisation and Warfare' conference, Centre for Sustainable Urban and Regional Futures, Manchester, November 2002, organised by Simon Marvin and Steve Graham.

4. Shimon Naveh, 'Dicta Clausewitz: Fractal Manoeuvre, A Brief History of Future Warfare in Urban Environments', address given in 'States of Emergency: The Geography of Human Rights', a debate that formed part of *Territories Live*, 5 November 2004, Btzalel Gallery, Tel Aviv.

5. Lieutenant-General John P. Abizaid, *Doctrine for Joint Urban Operations*, Joint Publication 3-06, 16 September 2002, available at www.nyt.com (accessed September 2002).

6. Marvin, 'Military Urban Research Programmes'.

7. Derek Gregory, *The Colonial Present*, Oxford: Blackwell, 2004, p. 201.

8. Stephen Graham, 'Switching Societies Off: War, Infrastructure, Geopolitics', draft published at http://www.geography.dur.ac.uk/s.d.n.graham.

9. Mike Davis, 'The Pentagon as Global Slumlord', a project of the Nation Institute. See www.tomdispatch.com (accessed 12 April 2004).

10. Srdjan Jovanovic Weiss, 'NATO as Architectural Critic', www.cabinetmagazine.org, 1 (Winter 2000/01). Weiss describes the way in which, during the bombing campaign, General Wesley Clark divided targets into 'strategic' and 'tactical'. Besides air defence, military forces, supply roads, and command and control objects, strategic targets included 'sustaining infrastructure and resources'. This comprised urban targets, infrastructure, bridges, electrical plants and oil refineries, but also administrative buildings. Weiss describes the five-step target selection procedure that was continually presented to the public: '1. Targets are suggested at NATO's headquarters in Brussels as well as in Germany and Italy. 2. A cell in the Pentagon called J-2T studies the feasibility of the target. 3. The planners measure the strategic value of a target against the drawbacks. 4. Lawyers at the Pentagon and at NATO's headquarters work on justifying the targets. 5. Presidents of major NATO countries review the target list.'

11. At the conference 'Cities as Strategic Sites: Militarisation, Anti-Globalisation and Warfare', Centre for Sustainable Urban and Regional Futures, Manchester, November 2002.

12. Davis, 'The Pentagon as Global Slumlord'.

13. Palestinian armed organisations killed more than 80 Israeli civilians between 1 March and 1 April 2002. www. amnesty.org (accessed 12 February 2003).

14. Stephen Graham, 'Constructing Urbicide by Bulldozer in the Occupied Territories', in Stephen Graham, *Cities, War and Terrorism*, Oxford: Blackwell, 2004, p. 332.

15. Graham, 'Constructing Urbicide', p. 334.

16. Eyal Weizman, Nadav Harel and Anselm Franke, a filmed conversation with Brigadier-General Aviv Kokhavi, 15 October 2004.

17. Hannan Greenberg, 'The Limited Conflict: This is How You Trick Terrorists', www.ynet.co.il (accessed 23 March 2004).

18. See the complete Rome Statute of the International Criminal Court at http://www.un.org./law/icc/statute/romefra.htm.

19. Rome Statute.

20. Gideon Levy, 'Tank Lanes Built Between New Jenin Homes', *Ha'aretz*, 10 May 2004.

21. See Eyal Weizman, Nadav Harel and Anselm Franke, *Project Jenin*, 2004, a short documentary discussion with the civil engineers responsible for the reconstruction.

22. RMA (Revolution in Military Affairs) is the adaptation of military organisation to fit developments in the technological, economic and political spheres since the Cold War. The reorganisation includes far-reaching changes in military planning, equipment, training, and ultimately the ability to wage war. It seeks the technological evolution of weapons and information technology to fit military tasks in times of the decline of the nation state and an emerging international order.

23. See Greenberg, 'The Limited Conflict'.

24. See Colonel Eric M. Walters, 'Stalingrad, 1942: With Will, Weapon, and a Watch', in Colonel John Antal and Major Bradley Gericke (eds), *City Fights*, New York: Ballantine Books, 2003, p. 59.

25. See Walters, 'Stalingrad', p. 72.

26. The issue of simultaneity is best summed up by the following quotation from General Charles C. Krulak: 'In one moment in time, our service members will be feeding and clothing displaced refugees – providing humanitarian assistance. In the next moment, they will be holding two warring tribes apart – conducting peacekeeping operations. Finally, they will be fighting a highly lethal mid-intensity battle. All on the same day, all within three city blocks. It will be what we call the three block war.' www.urbanoperations.com (accessed 21 April 2003).

27. The system has its beginning with what General von Moltke of the Wehrmacht called *Auftragstaktik* (mission-oriented tactics). See Martin Van Creveld, *Command in War*, Cambridge: Harvard University Press, 1985, p. 270, and General Amos Yadlin, 'Urban Warfare from the Air', *Ma'arachot*, 384 (July 2002), p. 31.

28. Manuel DeLanda, *War in the Age of Intelligent Machines*, New York: Zone Books, 1991, pp. 78–79.

29. This situation led to the fact that the developments of the battle were understood at the soldiers' homes long before they were reported by the mainstream news. I personally remember rather bizarre situations such as receiving live information through the mobile phone of one of my colleagues whose friend was taking part in the battle.

30. Sharon Rotbard, 'The War of Streets and Homes', lecture delivered at the IAUA conference, Tel Aviv, 2000.

31. The IDF battalion Duvdevan ('cherry' in Hebrew) is the IDF's Special Forces undercover unit designed to operate in the Occupied Territories. *Mista'arvim* is the Hebrew term for 'becoming an Arab': soldiers fight in jeans, shirts and sneakers, they can often speak Arabic, know how to apply stage make-up and often drill in a mock-up West Bank city. A typical team consists of eight soldiers. Out of 10 commanders the units had, no less than eight were either court-martialled or relieved of their commands due to excessive, unnecessary force against Palestinian civilians.

32. See Amnon Brazilay, 'This Time They're Not Preparing for the Last War', *Ha'aretz*, 17 April 2004, and Zuri Dar and Oded Hermoni, 'Israeli Start-Up Develops Technology to See Through Walls',

Ha'aretz, 1 July 2004. See also Amir Golan, 'The Components of the Ability to Fight in Urban Areas', *Ma'arachot*, 384 (July 2002), p. 97.

33. Conversation with Ze'ev Schiff, 15 October 2002, Tel Aviv.

34. Marshal Berman, 'Falling Towers: City Life After Urbicide', in Dennis Crow (ed.), *Geography and Identity*, Washington: Maisonneuve Press, 1996, pp. 172–92.

35. See Graham, 'Constructing Urbicide'.

36. Graham, 'Constructing Urbicide', p. 333.

Discussion (edited extracts)

Declan McGonagle Thank you very much. I think that's been another incredibly rich presentation which I think will stimulate a lot of discussion. Could I ask Anna and Eyal to come back to the table and we can take some questions…

In a lot of our strategic discussion over the last year we were concerned with the risk of the Biennial becoming one-dimensionalised in its relationship with the funding processes and the funding realities through which these projects have to work, if they're going to exist at all. The judgment has to be made whether to actually inhabit that tension between a series of agendas – or a series of tensions between different and differing agendas. It seems to me to be part of the responsibility not just of practitioner artists or curators but also of organisations like the Biennial to inhabit those tensions and not to walk away from them. To negotiate a role for art if we feel that art has some sort of value in the world.

Anna Minton This is the first time I've had anything to do with biennials, and I just wonder how transparent to the participants the economics of the Biennial are. At the end of the day, these are not only political and cultural policy issues, but are grounded in economic decisions. I mean how much comes from the public sector for example, how much from the private sector?

Declan McGonagle Lewis, do you want to pick that up?

Lewis Biggs It's, let's say, two thirds policy following the general government or regional or city agendas and it's one third private trusts, but obviously private trusts also have their own agendas to do with educational objectives. Every penny of money that the Biennial uses has a string attached to a policy, so the Biennial is supported by a network of public money policies and so… if this is the answer to your transparency list?

Anna Minton Well, I want more. What are the policies? What are the strings? Which departments are involved?

Lewis Biggs It's to do with regeneration agendas and it's to do with marketing agendas. That's to say, maybe a third of the total budget comes from the Regional Development Agency, specifically in order to market Liverpool as a location for investment and as a location for cultural tourism, and the ability of the Biennial to attract that funding is quantified specifically by how many businesses relocate or how many cultural tourists come to the city. The regeneration agenda is much harder to define, but there is a belief that because of artists' activities, the areas of the city where people are prepared to walk at night are expanding. That is good for the city, and the properties where the artists show their work will rise in value and investors and developers will therefore have the confidence to make that bit of the city work… you know, this is standard stuff, it's not rocket science.

Declan McGonagle This question does come up quite often in this sort of context, and often seems predicated on the idea that art was somehow innocent of all of this in the past. Which is just not true. Art has always been part of the socio-economic transactional processes in society. They are cast in particular ways now, and it's down to us, it seems to me, to be confident and to consciously enter that negotiation process and position what we believe to be of value in the foreground. There is a pattern of art processes being disempowered because art didn't consciously enter that negotiation.

Eyal, could I bring you in here in relation to the idea of what responsibility artists or architects have… your exhibition *A Civilian Occupation* was banned by the Association of Architects. Was that because you named something that they did not want to have in the public realm?

Eyal Weizman No. Actually, what happened there was a complex scenario. The Association of Architects has a bit of an old-fashioned perception of the profession and did not want to associate themselves with a kind of artistic production with human rights violations, with war crimes etc. The problem was exactly this kind of implicit connection between creative practices and repercussions that they have, and I think it relates to that debate here because they wanted to remain rather aloof from the whole situation. Most of the stuff in the exhibition had been published before in a human rights report that I did… OK, it had a big effect, but it was already out. It was that kind of internal disciplinary crisis and somehow it was the last in the series of disciplinary crises in Israel. It's nothing more than that, which was actually done by a lot of PhD students who returned from the US and Europe to Israel and started to say, archaeology is political, and the way we are teaching history is political, and education is political. Breaking down the political power structure behind different disciplines. And, you know, they fell one after the other, and somehow architecture was the last. I mean there was no big deal. What's the big deal? That we don't know the settlements of the West Bank, we don't know the human rights abuses, it was that kind of internal shock.

Anna, I was just wondering about your suggestions at the end, which I find fascinating and robust and all that. But I'm just wondering if they don't imply another order of exclusion. Because – take me, I'm a foreigner, I'm living in London, what affordable housing am I ever going to get and from whom? In a sense it creates another sort of barrier. What percentage of Londoners are not British citizens?

Anna Minton I don't know, but I would have thought it's quite high.

Eyal Weizman And how excluded are we from the whole set of welfare and public benefits? I mean why should we actually fight for that kind of affordability when the national barrier is still so strong and the citizenship barrier is so strong, and is not really addressing anything that is at the heart of multiculturalism or encouraging it? So we can say that's a stage, but perhaps the focus should be somewhere else and perhaps by actually reinforcing some strands – and I'm not saying everything in the welfare state – you actually create barriers to immigration and in that respect to the ability of a city to absorb immigration. So... I mean, that's another level of exclusion.

Anna Minton Yes, I think that's a good point.

■ ■ ■ ■ ■ ■ ■ ■

Eyal Weizman What about broadening this into the wider role of public funding, how does it insert art in society? What kind of biennial could there be or would it be called a biennial, for example, if artistic work was aimed at pleasure for children, nothing to do with attracting foreign capital, foreign investment to create further jobs, if public money was aimed at creation? Art workshops, potteries in deprived parts of Liverpool. What is at the back of my mind is something that you said, Anna. You said, look, neo-liberalism is here at least for the short term. I think that this kind of discussion mustn't censor itself politically because there are and there have been alternatives. I remember going to a wonderful exhibition in New York, which was about the period of Roosevelt. This was at the height of social democracy, but there was a policy to fund unemployed artists to do art because it said you are better at doing art than sweeping the streets. This goes back to discussions within the Greater London Council in the eighties about the way in which public funding can in some way be accountable to the community. Then of course, Thatcherism came in and any public funding would simply be pump priming in order to create spaces to invest in, to attract tourists and investment. I think the issue has to be up for grabs again in terms of examining very fundamental political assumptions and daring to question them. Saying, we don't think this policy has to be forever. We question it because it is creating a very frightening world.

Anna Minton Limiting it to public funding for the arts. It is a contentious issue – and I'm sure there are lots of people in the audience who know more about it than I do – but the direction that public funding for arts is taking and the sorts of things that curators have to do in order to get money for their projects is causing a lot of anger in the art world. For example, in relation to issues of community engagement, it seems artists are now used as tools of regeneration. If they say they are going to work with communities to do x, y and z they'll get funding, but if they're doing something which is more 'art for art's sake' they're less likely to get funding. The thrust of central policy is neo-liberal, we shouldn't rail about it but try and slip things in where we can, and be consistently aware of the tensions.

Declan McGonagle There is enormous investment in Western European societies in the model of production and distribution, absolutely huge. There has been a rhetoric and some funding allocated in recent years to social practices, which was criticised as instrumentalism in terms of social inclusion and so forth. But the balance of power, power and powerlessness, has not actually changed in society. Third-level education is still fundamentally predicated on preparing the signature artist, that is how one accesses value in our society as an artist. The alternative is a much more participatory or collaborative practice as an artist, and I am not talking about community arts. In fact, I would argue that the terminology and the thinking of community arts needs to be put aside because it was self-marginalising. The profession that I am part of has been very, very bad – in these islands if not further afield – in coming up with the language and the argument to persuade this society as a whole, not just the politicians, that this process we're engaged in has value. We have not persuaded the public; the public distrust this process. There is a story of Damien Hirst, about to see a contemporary sculpture exhibition with his mother. And he noticed that his mother was extremely suspicious of the experience, distrusted the transaction totally, and yet on the way home she had to go to a chemist's shop to buy some medication, and he noted that she completely trusted the transaction in the chemist's shop. Yet, if that had gone wrong, it could have literally been lethal. And there's that difference, this is why Damien Hirst started to make those early pieces using drug cabinets and so forth. He wanted to literally step into that transactional space which he saw his mother had complete trust in, whereas the art space she deeply distrusted. It's the curatorial profession process, which stands in the space between artist and non-artist, which has failed in that regard. We have failed and we won't be able to do anything about it until we acknowledge our failure, and then move on from that position. Now, I mean it's worth arguing that, but I actually believe that. If we persuade the society the politicians will roll in behind.

■ ■ ■ ■ ■ ■ ■ ■ ■

Declan McGonagle We have a question about the writers and their role in the peace process in Northern Ireland. It's hard to know where to start in this sense but it can be tracked. There was a particular moment in the late sixties, when this particular phase of the Irish troubles – they had been going on for about 800 years – really kicked off following the civil rights campaign. It actually seemed to surprise that generation that things could degenerate from what some people described as a lovely wee country into sectarian violence in the early seventies to the degree it took place. Many of the issues depended on where you positioned your cultural identity. You adhered to a political system in relation to the statement you would make about your cultural identity first. For example, I am Catholic, nationalist, therefore... and a lot of people had to step back and say, well, does my claiming the status of Catholic nationalist mean that I have to approve of people being bombed, for instance? Is it possible to have an identity and claim it, but not approve of violence? The drama acted out and crystallised issues for many people, and there were many people who were very confused. The debate started within the Catholic community first, about do you agree with violence or do you not agree with violence. That became articulated very consciously among a generation of writers, particularly poets but also playwrights. What was explored was the way in which language supported a foundation myth about cultural identity, and the way in which cultural practice supported that myth which in one respect was leading to people being bombed in the city centre, in shops in Belfast. And it was the unacceptability of that, I think, that led artists to take responsibility for that foundation myth claim and to examine it, to pull it right back to that foundation myth and then try and construct another possible way of living in that place. It happened much later within the loyalist community because the loyalist community was connected to the State and was apparently connected to power and didn't feel it had to question its own identity. But that has gone on latterly within the loyalist community and one of the things that's very hard to see at the moment is the confusion that exists within the loyalist community, because it did not engage and it did not literally have the writers who carried out that investigation – and I'm not being sectarian in saying that. It has been much discussed and much documented that the nationalist community had a generation of writers – not visual artists, very interestingly. Traditional visual culture is distributed much more slowly and has much more difficulty in getting out there to a wider constituency, which is not the case with literary culture. But what happened since the peace process has become a reality – I don't mean that we have peace, I mean that the process has become a reality – is that there has been a lot of attention by visual artists to the idea of public space, not just the object in public space, but the public realm and what that means. That has tripped over into issues of civil space and citizenship and the idea of participation and there is a generation of artists working transnationally, I would say, but particularly in the north, without the support of a private market system, where participation is key, where the artist is seen as a negotiator and the art space is seen as a space of negotiation and not a passing on of authority. And that challenges the inherited model, the nineteenth-century model, and asks for a new model of production and distribution to be put in place. But it started – and this can be shown historically, that the language that was used in the document called the Good Friday Agreement owed a huge amount to the way that language was literally stretched, the meaning of the language was literally stretched by the poets, and politicians. We held an event in Dublin with a number of politicians where the writing of the agreement was discussed as a cultural act, because it dealt absolutely with foundation myth. And because of the fact that it had, there were multiple readings possible. There is one writing, and there was an attempt to efface it by another writing, but, in fact, both narratives were visible. And there was a phrase that was coined in the peace process which was crucially important, which was 'parity of esteem'. And the peace process only became effective when it was accepted by both sides that victory or defeat was not the issue, it was parity of esteem from both cultures. Parity, not saying it's the same but saying it has equal value, it's different so it's an acceptance of difference etc. etc. Sorry, I've spoken longer than I intended, you were asked that question…

Eyal Weizman I see the parallels between the Israel and Palestine conflict and its kind of territorial and political problems with other such – I dare say – frontiers. It's amazing how much there is in common and how much somehow there is still kind of a paradigm of partition that is so strong when you come to speak about the Israeli/Palestinian conflict. It has this British colonial tradition to it, but it has no grounding in effect; it has never worked in any sort of colonial environment, the geography just does not lend itself to partition. And I think that what I'm trying to do, rather than propose something immediately different, is to show that very simple kind of paradigm that says, OK, we can partition it, OK, you want to partition it, this is what you want, this is what you'll get. You'll get islands, you'll get bridges, because this is how it is everywhere that you have this kind of overlap of cultural claims. Now Israel and Palestine are not two separate places, they are basically two different readings of the same place, so how can you separate them? How can you separate that cultural connection to the same environment? I think we have to quickly move away from the two-state solution as the only thing that we can imagine as a way to a future. In fact, how to get there is only through failure. You want to divide, and you'll get these islands if the road map is followed and Israel retreats: there'll be Israeli sovereign islands in Palestine and Palestinian sovereign islands within Israeli control. Those will be the Trojan horses that will finally erode this sort of crystal sphere of sovereignty which extends above and below. You need those mechanisms in order to do it and I always think that failure is the best way to get there: some of your country is below mine and some of mine is below yours and the air is connected and finally it will just collapse from its own kind of weight of complexity. The problems in Northern Ireland and Israel are particular local problems as well as having wider resonances. Israel and Palestine operate as a laboratory for different processes and have had a gearing effect on a lot of international politics in the second half of the twentieth century. A simple crossing of Sharon onto the other side of the canal triggered a whole kind of global process, magnified through international politics. To understand Israel and Palestine, it is very productive to think about it as a laboratory, to understand the whole process of mimicry and to analyse how the different military technologies have migrated from Israel/Palestine to Iraq, to Afghanistan, to different open frontiers in the 'war on terrorism'. In a sense this crisis of sovereignty, which is the Israeli/Palestinian crisis, is a global crisis.

■ ■ ■ ■ ■ ■ ■ ■

You judge temporality not through the proof of time, because temporality is a state of the present. You know it can be short, it could be long, but it could be forever. As far as the Palestinians are concerned, since 1948 we have had four generations living in a temporary state. So the extension of the state of temporality is offering a particular political mode. In a war of terror, it offers the suspension of some rights because it is a temporary state and we have an emergency. And it's a very effective definition of the present, however long it may be, we could have a permanent state of temporality that allows us to do things which would otherwise not be accepted. Temporality allowed them [Palestinians] to be extra-territorial as well as right. In places the camps become extra-territorial and therefore agents of a different sort of sovereignty, and I think that one needs to look at those as potential. It is an incredibly powerful insistence by Palestinians on this temporality: the fact that it is not a city, it's a camp, is an incredible agent of change in the Middle East.

Contributors

Notes on Contributors

Giorgio Agamben is a professor of aesthetics at the University of Verona, Italy. His many publications include *The Coming Community*, *Homer Sacer* and recently *State of Exception*.

Irina Aristarkhova is assistant professor at the National University of Singapore University Scholars' Programme and the School of Computing, where she directs the Cyberarts Research Initiative.

Ole Bouman moderated the second Manifesta Coffee Break, *Who is the Host?*. He is editor in chief of *Volume* and co-curated Manifesta 3, Ljubljana, 2000. (www.archis.org)

Nicolas Bourriaud is director of Palais de Tokyo, Paris and curator of Biennale de Lyon 2005. His book *Relational Aesthetics* was translated into English in 2002. (www.palaisdetokyo.com)

Iaroslava Boubnova co-curated the Moscow Biennale 2004. She is the founding director of the Institute of Contemporary Art, Sofia, and was curator of Manifesta 4, Frankfurt, 2002. She is a board member of International Foundation Manifesta (IFM).

Chris Dercon moderated the first Manifesta Coffee Break, *Refugee*. Since 2003 he has been director of Haus der Kunst, Munich. He is a former board member of IFM. (www.hausderkunst.de)

Paul Domela is deputy chief executive of Liverpool Biennial. He coordinated the Manifesta Coffee Breaks and edited this publication. (www.biennial.com)

Dieter Lesage teaches philosophy at the department for Audiovisual and Dramatic Arts (RITS) at the Erasmus University Brussels. He recently published (in Dutch) *Vertoog over verzet. Politiek in tijden van globalisering* (2004).

Bruce Mau is director of Bruce Mau Design. He wrote *An Incomplete Manifesto for Growth* in 1998. In 2004, he produced *Massive Change: The Future of Global Design*, together with the Institute without Boundaries. (www.brucemaudesign.com; www.massivechange.com)

Declan McGonagle moderated the third Manifesta Coffee Break, *Occupation: Unknown*. He is Professor of Art and Design at the University of Ulster and director of Interface (Centre for Research in Art, Technologies and Design). He is chair of the board of Liverpool Biennial. (www.interface.ulster.ac.uk)

Anna Minton is a freelance journalist and writer focusing on social policy. She is a regular contributor to *The Guardian*, *The Sunday Times*, and Shelter's magazine *ROOF*.

Anna Pollert is Professor of Sociology of Work at the London Metropolitan University Working Lives Research Institute. *Transformation at Work in the New Market Economies of Central Eastern Europe* was published in 1999.

Eyal Weizman is an architect based in Tel Aviv and London. The exhibition and the publication *A Civilian Occupation: The Politics of Israeli Architecture*, which he edited and curated together with Rafi Segal, were banned by the Israeli Association of Architects, but later shown as an ongoing project in New York, Berlin, Rotterdam, Malmö and other places. He is currently developing his project *The Politics of Verticality* into a book and a film.

Participants

Ami Barak (curator, Paris)
Lewis Biggs (chief executive, Liverpool Biennial)
Luchezar Boyadjiev (artist, Sofia)
Iaroslava Boubnova (founding director, ICA, Sofia; curator, Manifesta 4, Frankfurt)
Phil Collins (artist, Belfast)
Wilfried Cooreman (collector, Brussels)
Chris Dercon (director, Haus der Kunst, Munich)
Paul Domela (deputy chief executive, Liverpool Biennial)
Hedwig Fijen (founding director, Manifesta 1; director, International Foundation Manifesta, Amsterdam)
Lourdes Fernandez (coordinator, Manifesta 5, San Sebastian)
Martin Fritz (director, Das Festival der Regionen 2005, Linz; general coordinator, Manifesta 4, Frankfurt)
Massimiliano Gioni (curator, Berlin Biennale 2006; curator, Manifesta 5, San Sebastian)
Christoph Grunenberg (director, Tate Liverpool)
Marieke van Hal (general coordinator, International Foundation Manifesta, Amsterdam)
Jeanne van Heeswijk (artist, Rotterdam)
Maaretta Jaukkuri (professor, Art in Common Space, Trondheim Academy of Fine Art)
Marta Kuzma (curator, Manifesta 5, San Sebastian)
Dieter Lesage (philosopher, Brussels)

Henry Meyric Hughes (president, AICA; president, International Foundation Manifesta, London)
Viktor Misiano (editor, *Manifesta Journal*; curator, Manifesta 1, Rotterdam)
Stephanie Moisdon-Trembley (director, BVD, Paris; curator, Manifesta 4, Frankfurt)
Michiel Nagelhout (accountant, International Foundation Manifesta)
Deimantas Narkevicius (artist, Vilnius)
Katalyn Neray (director, Ludwig Museum of Contemporary Art, Budapest; curator, Manifesta 1)
Lioba Reddeker (director, Basis Wien, Vienna)
Lilijana Stepancic (director, International Graphic Arts Centre, Ljubljana)
Damon Tidman (artist, Liverpool)
Ramon Tio Bellido (secretary-general, AICA, Paris)
Barbara Vanderlinden (director, Roomade, Brussels; curator, Manifesta 2, Luxembourg)
Mechtild Widrich (publisher, Vienna)
Igor Zabel (curator, Museum Ljubljana; coordinator, Manifesta 3, Ljubljana)

Irina Aristarkhova (assistant professor, National University Singapore)
Zdenka Badovinac (director, Moderne Galerija Ljubljana)
Fabianne Bernadini (Casino Luxembourg)
Lewis Biggs (chief executive, Liverpool Biennial)
Waling Boers (director, BüroFriedrich, Berlin)
Iaroslava Boubnova (founding director, ICA, Sofia; curator, Manifesta 4, Frankfurt)
Ole Bouman (chief editor, *Volume*, Rotterdam; curator, Manifesta 3, Ljubljana)
Nicolas Bourriaud (director, Palais de Tokyo, Paris)
Ana Devic (WHW Curators' Collective, Zagreb)
Paul Domela (deputy chief executive, Liverpool Biennial)
Hedwig Fijen (founding director, Manifesta 1; director, International Foundation Manifesta, Amsterdam)
Elena Filipovic (editor, Manifesta Book, Brussels)
Robert Fleck (director, Deichtorhalle, Hamburg; curator, Manifesta 2, Luxembourg)
Dirk Fleischmann (artist, Frankfurt am Main)
Martin Fritz (director, Das Festival der Regionen 2005, Linz; coordinator, Manifesta 4, Frankfurt)
Marieke van Hal (managing editor, *Manifesta Journal*, Amsterdam)
Anders Harm (curator, Kunsthoone, Tallinn)
Erna Hecey (Gallery Hecey, Luxembourg)
Arne Hendrikx (Casco, Rotterdam)
Maria Hlavajova (director, BAK, Utrecht; curator, Manifesta 3, Ljubljana)
Kathy Rae Huffmann (director of visual art, Cornerhouse, Manchester)
Stefan Kalmar (director, Kunstverein Munich)

Boris Kremer (Künstlerhaus Bethanien, Berlin)
Enrico Lunghi (director, Casino Luxembourg; coordinator, Manifesta 2, Luxembourg)
Henry Meyric Hughes (president, AICA; president, International Foundation Manifesta, London)
Louli Michaelidou (cultural officer, Ministry of Education and Culture, Nicosia)
Lioba Reddeker (director, Basis Wien, Vienna)
Vanessa Joan Muller (curator, Frankfurt Kunstverein)
Hanno Soans (curator, Museum of Modern Art, Tallinn)
Lilijana Stepancic (director, International Graphic Arts Centre, Ljubljana)
Yiannis Toumazis (director, Nicosia Art Centre)
Stephanie Moisdon-Trembley (director, BVD, Paris; curator, Manifesta 4, Frankfurt)
Willem Velthoven (director, Mediamatic; professor, Universität der Künste, Berlin)
Jochen Volz (curator, Portikus, Frankfurt)
Neil White (artist, The Arts Catalyst, London)
Thomas Wulffen (art critic, Berlin)
Igor Zabel (curator, Museum Ljubljana; coordinator, Manifesta 3, Ljubljana)

Cecilia Andersson (curator, Werk Ltd, Liverpool)
Matei Bejenaru (director, Vector Cultural Association, Iasi)
Lewis Biggs (chief executive, Liverpool Biennial)
Iaroslava Boubnova (founding director, ICA, Sofia; curator, Manifesta 4, Frankfurt)
Thomas Boutoux (art critic and independent curator, Paris)

Laura Britton (curator, public programmes, Tate Liverpool, Liverpool)
Wong Hoy Cheong (artist, Kuala Lumpur)
Paul Domela (deputy chief executive, Liverpool Biennial)
Dirk Fleischmann (artist, Frankfurt am Main)
Rainer Ganahl (artist, New York)
Marieke van Hal (managing editor, *Manifesta Journal*, Amsterdam)
Jeanne van Heeswijk (artist, Rotterdam)
Hans Hemmert (artist, Berlin)
Arne Hendriks (Casco, Utrecht)
Kathy Rae Huffman (director of visual art, Cornerhouse, Manchester)
Gareth Hughes (artist, Liverpool)
Florian Kossak (co-op member, Glasgow Letters on Architecture and Space, Glasgow)
Sebastian Khourian (architect, TOOAUP [The Office of Alternative Urban Planning], Barcelona)
Steven Lane (artist, Liverpool)
Francesco Manacorda (independent critic and curator, London)
Declan McGonagle (director, Interface, University of Ulster, Belfast)
Louli Michaelidou (cultural officer, Ministry of Education and Culture, Nicosia)
Anna Minton (writer, London)
Michael Panayiotis (artist, Nicosia)
Anna Pollert (professor of Sociology of Work, Working Lives Research Institute, London Metropolitan University, London)
Angelika Richter (director, Werkleitz Gesellschaft, Halle)
Marko Sancanin (architect, Platforma 9,81, Zagreb)
Tatjana Schneider (co-op member, Glasgow Letters on Architecture and Space, Glasgow)
Imogen Stidworthy (artist, Liverpool)

Christine Tohme (director, The Lebanese Association for Plastic Arts – Ashkal Alwan, Beirut)
Yiannis Toumazis (general coordinator, Manifesta 6, Nicosia)
Stefanos Tsivopoulos (artist, Amsterdam)
Martin Vincent (director, The Annual Programme, Manchester)
Marina Vishmidt (writer, editor, artist, London)
Stevan Vukovic (Visual Art Programs Coordinator, SKC, Belgrade)
Eyal Weizman (architect, London/Tel Aviv)
Chin-tao Wu (Institute of European and American Studies, Taipeh)
Bozidar Zrinski (curator, International Centre of Graphic Arts, Ljubljana)